7 WHYS

A PATH TO FIND YOURSELF.

MONALISHA PANI

Made with ♥ on the Notion Press Platform
www.notionpress.com

7 whys

The Path to Find Yourself

TO EVERY PERSON WHO IS UNABLE TO FIND THEMSELVES.

Written By- Monalisha Pani

Edited By- Payel Atta

Contents

Foreword

INTRODUCTION

Hello readers, this is my very first attempt in the creative field of writing novels. This first novel of mine is based on my life experiences, being a girl of 20, I have used all my best knowledge to help you brighten up your day. I have intended to share a number of ideas that we can easily apply to our lives. Here I aim to plant a few more seeds of humanity, positivity and radiance in the society. Love and harmony are all that we want to get life sorted but there are so many complications of thoughts that are keeping us away from that beautiful world that it certainly appears to be a dream for many of us. Life is proving to be a struggle more than a journey, so let's find out what is keeping us away from the goodness of life and how can we make through them.

Here I wish to help my readers relive their lives in the best splendid way by helping them to release themselves from anything that is holding them back or making their life uneasy in some way. Being an inexperienced writer, I am trying hard to present my ideas in the most appealing manner hoping to provide you the delightful experience of reading a novel based on common idea of life. I beg your understanding for my first work and I promise to improve my creative writing remarkably in my next work.

In this writing of mine I have shared certain ideas and thoughts that I have experienced to be useful in many arenas of life. I am willing to help the society move towards positivity and I have tried not to mention even a bit of negative ideas so as to keep my readers away from negativity as much as possible. Because even a slightest mention of negativity can turn the entire attempt worthless. Our mind works in desired manner and relates better when put in one single direction and not when multiple paths are projected without proper guidance. It is too delicate to handle tough complicated explanation as sometimes it moves in that exact path which was mentioned not to be taken. We should allow only to focus on what to get done and not at all on what should not be done.

We live in a society where expressing our weaknesses and traumas is considered as fragile excuses, where every day we are getting judged for who we are and somewhere at some point this is considered as normal, many of us are suffering from stress, anxiety, depression, past traumas etc. I mean to say everyone is dealing with some kind of negative energy in one way or another. Ranges may be different but impacts are almost alike, each one of us are precious and each one of us needs to get protected. So here I am wishing to convey how can we protect ourselves from a list of negative energies by demonstrating what power we hold within us. Protection is not something we should seek for it needs to be created in our mind by analysing the power of the universe.

This is a small work of encouragement to look at the stars shinning bright on you, the sun throwing all its love rays at you to confess the love of universe for you and remind you that you are never alone. I want you to observe every positive thing happening in your surrounding so as to lift you up & make you understand the meaning of every moment of life. I want you to learn the value of each moment of life in order to realise and reach where you need to be that is your soul purpose.

I want you to understand that the what you are, the way you are is also determined by the universe and you have to accept yourself no matter what then why not euphorically. We need to learn to accept certain things and need to let off the control of certain things those are beyond our control and just live a carefree and happy life.

I want to say,

"Don't look out for wings to fly,
feel the wind at your height,
and give a bright smile to let
It pass-through your gums."

I hope my piece of work will elevate your life and upgrade you at a spiritual level. Here I have directly addressed to my readers as it is a general life-based novel.

I hope you can find your comfort here. I hope you will recognise your home and its vitality after reading this. I wish you to reach home.

I hope you will be ready to embrace positivity after going through my novel.

I am asking you to go through my novel with an open mind, without giving much stress to the so-called rules and restrictions set in the world. Let it just gently pass through your mind.

Preface

This book is completely oriented on a single dialogue from Mrs. Warren's Profession written by George Bernard Shaw :

"People are always blaming the circumstances for what they are.

I don't believe in circumstances. The people who got into this world are the people who get up and look for circumstances they want , and if they can't find them, they make them ."

Acknowledgements

ACKNOWLEDGEMENTS

Hi all,

I can't possibly thank everyone who have helped me to experience all these feelings that I have come across. But I will mention some of them – Miss Payel Atta, Miss Debashree Das, Miss Pratisha Patra, Miss Ratnamalini Pani all of them have been with me all through the small journey of my life and have witnessed me getting stronger and softer day by day, and are aware of how I have made it to this. No doubt all of them have played a major role to encourage me while writing this, Miss Payel is my first reader and editor of this novel she is the one who stood like a rock for me while working on this. This work would not have been possible without her providing me constant love and support. I thank Miss Ratna my elder sister for tolerating me for 20 years now and Miss Debashree for being my best friend since 2011 and she was the first person who saw my initial writing and said-"It is good work in it!". But I also want to thank every individual who have made me laugh while having teary eyes, who have made me go through both good and bad feelings because that is how I was able to find myself, my own starlight. I owe a huge thanks to this universe and my parents [Dr Dillip Kumar Pani and Mrs Sarita Pani], thank you for giving me this life on earth. Till now I haven't realised what is my soul's purpose but I can guarantee whatever it is I am ready to give my best in it, coz I can feel that flame in me. Here I want my readers to do the same that is feel that flame in you and work accordingly.

We all need to learn the path to find ourselves in the right manner because we can lose everybody else but our 'self' will be always with us to give us the experience of unconditional love that we seek from others. We are humans we need love of others but let's have a soft and spongy base of self-love ready for us so that every time we fail to get what we wished for we can still land softly on that base. There are so many reasons to stress about but let's choose to have a comfy air bag of self-love to lie on it when we are in mood of getting some rest. Let's learn our worth and value our 'self' in every unique and beautiful way available for us. We should learn our worth so that we won't end up having an unhappy life all throughout for not getting the desired level of love from others.

We all are moving towards something brighter than present, something lighter and smoother than what's now this is the flow of life. Even if we are not moving towards something brighter, we are still moving towards something that will be the reason for the brightness to enter into our lives with full force. Even if we are not stepping into a brighter world ahead, we are still moving close to that gateway that will open in itself for us at the divine timing.

Let's give it a try to recognise the path to find ourselves. Let's find out the right path to the 'self'.

Prologue

PROLOGUE

One night while I was about to sleep at, it was around 1AM when I came up with a though '*what about writing 7 whys.* It was just a sudden thought then I immediately gave it a google search if any book of such name exists already and thankfully, I didn't find any. Then slowly and silently many ideas and thoughts kept on peeking in my mind and that's how the novel is in your hands now. We all have many features those gradually grow with time to make us capable and responsible individuals. Maybe I am exploring those features of mine to find out where can I excel in future. I have never thought of getting into this field of writing novels and all, I was always someone who would focus more on academics than to develop some other talents or skills. But at the same time, I was also someone who would focus more on what I want rather than what others would suggest for me to be, but it was never working out straight for me. And now also this is so unexpected from a common girl like me to take a deep insight of life and share it through such a huge platform. No doubt today's generations are excelling in every other way of building a good career, hoping to find that platform of mine is proving a bit tough, but everything is worth trying. I hope this works out well for at least some of my readers to help them in some way.

First, I was writing it just for the sake of improving my writing skills and haven't thought of doing anything with it to make it public or show it to anyone, actually I was roaming around my home hiding it from time to time. But with the progress in the process of life it gradually turned in to something greater than I had expected it to be.

However, since its[this novel] birth it was a clear attempt to find out the deep sense of living life with connecting more with what we are. Since the very beginning it was an idea of finding out various concepts associated with seven particular questions.

I don't know what response I am going to get from this, it is really making me nervous. I wish it to positive, fingers crossed!

So, here is your starlight.

CHAPTER ONE

WHY DO WE EXPECT RESPECT FROM OTHERS?

Chapter 1

While we live in human society, we need to interact with different people to co-exist or meet our daily needs. We maintain various kinds of relation with people of different arenas of our life. Some places it is formal, somewhere it is cordial, somewhere affectionate and somewhere just ignorance. We generally wish to live a secure and happy life by maintaining good relation with people in our surroundings. We come across dissimilar kinds of people some are polite, some are not; some are considerate, some are not but the entire interaction depends on our personality also. Few are going to treat us with due respect while others may not do the same. While dealing with such individuals who doesn't know the right manner of treating people, we need to bring our maturity card into play whether polite one or rude one solely depends on our personality. We are the decision maker of the way we want the situation to turn out.

Almost in every situation of life the outcomes completely depend on our response to it. If we decide to stay pacific in a dispute it will end in a calm way, but if we decide to do the same outrageous activity as the other person it will turn into a bigger brawl than the previous one. I am not asking you to hold back your anger, I am asking you to not to get annoyed by anything, keep your mental peace in a stable state. It is not easy but we all know where there is a will there is a way. And by the moment you will start trying you will have already reached a superior level than that of now. We need to learn how to handle ourselves so as to live a peaceful and happy life.

Love everyone, respect everyone, treat everyone right but don't make people comfortable to insult you in any way and don't expect similar kind of treatment from them too, this will bring enormous peace and harmony within you. If you find anyone who is affecting your metal peace in adverse manner stay away as much as possible from that person. Stay away from those who are weak enough to treat you right. Keep yourself close with people of higher positive energy than yours because that is when you will realise life is so much more than just tolerating such weak individuals.

Life is a journey of learning, exploring and experiments with the things of the universe. Live it to the fullest because life is the most magical and wonderful gift of nature.

Be your own prince charming or princess Cinderella and love yourself like the limitless height of the sky. Create your own positive shield carry it as your wings, because you are the main character of your life story. Create your own idea of yourself in your mind by adding up your personality, behaviour, nature, good qualities, excellent qualities, beauty and everything else to enhance it every day with your daily growth. This idea of yourself in you will give you strength, consolation, motivation to not to give up every time. This idea of yours will never allow you to let yourself down in any situation, will give you the reason to be you and not afraid of anything. Keep it as your aim to be. You can feel the impact of this image from the very first day. This is going to give you merry feelings every single day.

If we expect to get treated in the right manner, we need to treat ourself right first. We need to learn- Who we are? What we wish for? What makes us happy? What sets fire in our soul? What excites us the most? What motivates us to work harder? What creates in us the latent heat of positivity? And many other undiscovered questions that we were ignoring till now, this will help us to learn how to treat ourself right.

Once we get this modification straight, we and people around us will realise this change and they will start looking at us with a new preferable perspective. And we can also consider it as your first step towards enlightenment of the idea of what success means to us. Yes, life is a journey and how to make the most out of this journey completely depends on our enlightened idea of success and happiness in us. Keep your purpose positive, work thrivingly, keep walking with positivity at heart and mind, and the best is yet to come.

The idea of you, in you, will lead you to do similar kind of activities as you see your future self in it. Those activities are mini steps in your path of acquiring that imaginary you in your mind. Shape your activities to shape your days and shape your days to shape your future. Start building yourself from the root level.

Chapter 2

Sometimes it is ok to be ourself, to be who we are in the present. Sometimes it is ok to just pass our days doing nothing just sleeping on our bed and facing all the imaginary bad and good situations. It's ok to be weak to be fragile at times. Remember growth is a process not a ladder to just climb on and on. We need to go back and forth in almost every step, sometimes we may find ourselves having no escape route other than just bearing that feeling of being helpless and that is how we evolve.

Don't consider these feeling as unnecessary or unwanted, don't divert yourself from facing them, these are the signs of your spiritual awakening. There will be days when you will feel like all your energies are getting drained whatever growth work you were doing on yourself just vanished and you are again at the starting point. This is a process and this is only how it works. Just try experiencing everything completely that is on your plate. Be with yourself, be there for yourself, take care of yourself regularly. We have our own pace different from one another, don't compare your growth will anyone because that will be the greatest disrespect that you can ever bring to yourself, live life at your own speed.

The day you were born was not an accident you were sent here with certain motive with an objective to contribute something to the human society. Anyhow you are going to do that one day or another and for that you will flourish at the right time set by the divine. Till then let the glorious sun rays nourish your dreams and desires, let the tempting rays of the stars show you the right direction. Keep walking forward, keep enhancing, keep flourishing just don't give up. And one day you will be capable enough of providing yourself everything that makes you happy, satisfies you and provides you utmost pleasure of life. What is meant for you is already making its way to you. Until then try to create the sense of completeness within you.

Stop expecting everything from everyone start believing in yourself. Search for the light within you, be your own light, embrace yourself tight, because not everyone you have faith in are going to be available for you always, hence keep your expectations to yourself, be self-dependent. The way we pass our days speaks a lot about us. The way we carry ourselves also conveys a lot about us. Complete your daily chores and make some time to brew a cup of coffee for yourself, sit relaxed, run your fingers on your cheeks and say you are worthy of every good thing that you desire for and give an ear to ear smile then go back to work with double enthusiasm and triple self-love. Create a fantastic and unique definition of elegance for yourself. Be that. Walk down on the path of self-dependence with effortless grace. Create your positive sphere around you that will filter out all evil forces and will attract only good energy to get into your bubble.

As humans what we need to make our day happiest is only a few loving words from our loved ones. A single quality moment with them is enough to make our day blissful. All we require is a little upthrust from them. But we can give that access to ourselves too. But that's completely a choice. Let's start to being there to lift ourselves up because not every day one of your loved one is going to kiss you on your forehead before you step out of your bed. As happiness is a state of mind and you are capable enough to make your day peerless. For example-work harder enjoy harder is my mantra of life. Create one for yourself and find delight and satisfaction in it.

Our mental thought processes, our way of perceiving things, our reactions to them signify who we are. And people around us treat us according to that only. And respect is something that should be earned right? So, let's keep our thoughts, perspectives and reactions as positive as possible. Let's prove ourselves as matchless in everything we can do. But if even after giving your best efforts you were not able to gain desired results, then at least you are not at complete fault. By the time you were giving your efforts you have already evolved yourself a bit more, you have already pulled yourself a step ahead and that's what matter the most- your self-growth. You learned something, you became a bit wiser, you rose up. You haven't given up. You came up. That's it. Celebrate.

We all gain experiences from things that doesn't give us our desired result. We should never consider our failures as things to worry about, as everyone needs a taste of failure to identify success.

Our mind is like a magnet, if we think about blessings, we attract them, if we think about problems, we attract them too. Yes, it is true that we can't control our mind every time but we can tilt it towards positivity and that is going to bring a commendable change in our lives. For example, if you believe in radiance of life then you will experience tremendous life changes in near future and if not, then, this normal life will continue until you discover its radiance. So always guide your mind to walk in a positive direction and things will start falling at your side one by one. Let's consider insult by higher authorities or respected family members as a positive thing as those are the sole reason of who we are or how perfect we are at things we do now-a-days. Hence it is only the thinking of the mind that controls our reactions and activities at respective situations. After you decide how to maintain your personality everything will seem in order to you.

Once you get to know about your comfortable personality trait then you can get a hold on yourself and regulate your mind a bit. That balance within you will create will create perfect image of yours in the minds of people you come across. This image will be considered as your societal image. Build respect for yourself in your heart and mind, don't leave it in the hands of others. Start realising your value, your positive traits, because from the day you will start walking after embracing all your positive power, the world is going to acknowledge your worth. But in order to receive this acknowledgement first you have take stand for yourself by being the first person to respect 'you'. The procedure is as follows- First explore your positive traits, your strength, your worth etc identify them and protect them. At second stage you need to work to enhance those good qualities in you. Thirdly you need to delete all possible negativity present in you. By now this procedure might be proving itself correct in some way and I assure you "Yes, it will", you just need to focus on yourself for some time to work it out.

You must be thinking it is not possible to eradicate all negative traits within oneself and exist in this world. But what if I say, yes, it is possible to remove all negative traits within you and survive in this world? When we work on our inner self and walking towards light by looking at it our only focus is reaching out to that light then it doesn't matter at all what surrounds us. We just keep pushing keep running towards our only aim of being a part of that radiance of mother earth. Once you start trying to remove almost all negativity the divine power will be standing outside the door to fill your life with magical love and excitement. The divine once observers your effort he will clear out all your blockages and will let all positivity surround you, to encourage you to keep moving forward. Trust the divine and put down your first step towards enlightenment and wisdom. Don't worry about how things will work turn out latter or how are you going to deal with people with evil forces, have fine trust on the greater power because he is the reason you are able to read this book today and he is going to be the reason of all your future successes and failures too.

Chapter 3

Whenever you are getting annoyed, irritated or distressed in over something then at that very moment look out for things which are direct blessings from the almighty such as your lifestyle, your dress for the day, your beauty, your healthy body and the most important one your breath and of course your healthy mind too. Celebrate all these blessings at once and put a smile on that beautiful face of yours. These efficacious thoughts will help you to gain control on yourself in unfavourable situations.

In most of the situations in life we are left with two paths one is easy path and other is right path. Our values, our morality and the proportion of humanity in us shows which path we should opt to take. Every time try walking on the right one because the right one seems difficult at present but brings tremendous happiness latter, and the easy one will make you feel comfortable at present but latter be prepared to pay the price. Be on the right path and trust that you will reap rewards at the end of the day. Keep up the good work.

Many a times in life we face individual who purposely intend to insult us with everything those individuals are meant to be forgiven without a second thought and those insults are meant to be thrown into the bin of your mind because they do that due certain insecurities, they feel inside them when they are around us. They think us superior from them in some way in virtue of which they try to repeatedly put us down. Treat such individual with love and care because deep down they are not happy with what they are. Hold their hand and try making them feel comfortable as much as possible on your part. Don't be too good on them just don't waste your energies or let them have their way to create some negativity within you. Keep the doors to your mind locked firmly here. Maintain healthy distance with love in mind as that love will keep our mind away from nourishing negativity produces by them.

If you have been working hard on something for a long time but your hard work is not paying off in terms of honour or finance, then don't build up some negative thoughts in your mind such as- why this is happening to me? Should I give up etc. as those thoughts will attract negative energy of the universe. Because universe has its own rules which are made for our highest good. It is going to repay for all your hard work and energy that you manifested for such a long duration along with highest interest, all at once.

No matter whatever hardships we are going through we need to have a laughing picture of ours saved in our mind to display it every time we think about our future so as to draw positive energy from it. Let's make a room in our mind to store all our good memories and achievements and call it our room of enchantment. So that every time we will open that door, we will forget all our worries by putting all our sweet teeny tiny huckleberries of blissful memories into them.

In happiness we get immersed into commemorating the situation by having parties we spend time in crowd but only sadness brings us closer to ourselves. It reminds us about our existence, emotions, feelings, views and experiences. It reminds us to embrace our self before anybody else. Distress moulds us to give us the best shape we need to acquire. While facing things we automatically learn how to deal with things like this and that we learn, we acquire, we unfold our wings to fly, fly high.

Whatever stage of life you are in may it be good or bad keep the keys of your happiness in your hands because that is too precious to lend it to anyone else. Don't let your mood to depend on how people treat you let it depend on what you think about yourself. Let's grow having an unmatchable kind of self-adoration and self-pampering.

Yes, for many of us respect matters the most, and we all work hard and study hard to earn respect only. Does that mean you can't be you? Then that respect is also not for you as you are not showing your genuine self to the world. And does that mean you need to keep impressing others? on what platform and why? Are they going to feed you every day? No, right?

Yes, give your best, work hardest, work smartest and simultaneously be there to love yourself because not everyone is going to appreciate you and your daily efforts towards life. The way we connect with our self, the things that keeps coming into our mind radiate and attract similar situations or circumstances or people. We need to focus on our intuition and vibes radiated by our soul in order to connect more with our self.

Reach out to the level of what you consider as your ideal self, reach that level of perfectness at your soul level. Acquire the best version of yourself, this is not something to be done in a matter of days or weeks this might take a year or two or even but at the end you will become your own lighthouse. And the joy of being your own light is like matching with the footsteps of almighty at certain times.

Chapter 4

Earlier I was suggesting respect needs to be earned and for that we need to learn from every passing moment. If something good happens in a day we need to examine that situation repeatedly from numerous dimensions and remember what exactly made it turn out so good, and if a bad day, then also we need to learn what made it bad was it us or someone else or something else, if it is us then we should bring the change within us if it is the other one as then we need to ask them to change or just create a boundary within us and them to avoid more awful days in near future. These modifications are vital for our improvement in every aspect of our lives. Learn, apply and flourish. Let's design our way of life through layout, references and views. Let's give it an architectural touch, let's make our life a marvellous one, let's enhance its grace with an exceptional fragrance. Bring out that magic stick in you and spell an excellent one on yourself, as you are also a part of divine consciousness.

Verifying our self is a talent that we need to build in ourself in order to gain required respect and admiration in society. However, self-satisfaction and soulful happiness matters the most in whatever we are doing. Yes, respect is important but first bring out our authentic self on the surface and then experience the true respect that we deserve. Everything that we do today, will plant the seeds for the future fortune tree. We need to be cautious in every single thing whether small or big no matter what. Hence let's sow the seeds of good deeds, self-growth, gratitude and patience and let's witness it to flourish right in front of our eyes.

The goodness of self-rectification

will enlighten up your life with knowledge and prosperity.

CHAPTER TWO

WHY DO WE DEARCH FOR HAPPY ENDINGS?

Chapter 1

Generally, while watching a movie or reading a story book we wish the story to end on a happy note, isn't it? But the question is why we do so? why the happiness of those characters matters so much to us? As humans we all carry a sympathetic and empathetic heart and a well-developed mind to react accordingly. And being the most blessed living being we carry the ability to provide comfort through our speech. Human life is a long journey of around 60 to 100 years and how can we even expect such a long journey without ups and downs. We fall, we crawl, we stand, we walk, we run & then the most amazing phase we fly higher and higher.

We all are aware that we face a certain number of hurdles in our respective lives. We go through difficulties that we haven't even dreamt about but the irony is whatever the problem is or how difficult it is to suffer we always come out of it with flying colours isn't it? All you have to do is believe in two persons, one is you yourself and the other is almighty. The very huge problem that seems as a mountain will appear as a plain surface to walk on in a matter of few weeks. It is just the matter of time that we are worried about. Everything comes to an end with time.

So, it is natural for us to wish for happy endings in movies while witnessing their problem scenes, because, we see a part of ourselves in them so we long for their forever happy life in the end. This shows how innocent human beings are or how loving we are for even reel characters, who doesn't even exist in reality. We are not able to realise how soft our heart is and how innocent our mind is, to perceive & feel the same suffering while reading or watching a drama. After all we are all humans along with the ability to feel we are gifted with the ability to think but we are not able to realise those are nothing but stories. We watch and read them because we know those are just dramas based on imagination but even after knowing that we desperately search for happy ending, because suffering or problem ends with time and a new beginning arrives, we trust this process consciously or subconsciously. We might not realise it in the very moment of witnessing problem scenes because we are so involved in the flow of the story. And the same goes for our real life too. We are so involved with problems of our daily lives that sometime we forget that time is something far more powerful than that of our problem.

So, whether it is reel or real every problem has an ending with time. And if we are wishing it to be a happy ending then we need to keep following the right path with all faith in the almighty. This will eventually lead us to our happy ending because no suffering is for forever. As like the director of a movie or writer of the story decides the fate or ending note of the characters, how the situation will turn out, what events will take place in their lives, how they are going to make through things and everything else. Similarly, God, the creator of the universe who is looking after two trillion galaxies all at once in each and every moment is the director or writer of our story. So, can you imagine how special you are. Can you imagine how blessed you are to have him as your director, no right? Take a moment to realise this basic fact that you are part of something so great than you can ever think of and feel the power of protection from such a mighty being. The divine power that looks after us, that teaches us lessons of life, that guides us in our soul's journey on earth is going to make us taste every aspects of life so that one day we can get merged with that divine power after learning enough, experiencing enough, witnessing enough and being wise enough.

Chapter 2

There will be times in which we will experience betrayal, get tormented even when we were just trying to be a benevolent individual. In these times we need to learn when to stop being good to others and start being with ourselves. At this phase of our life, you need to hold ourself back from just giving, trying and pleasing and have a look at ourself at our condition from just worrying about others what we have done to ourself. We need to turn around and start looking after ourself, hold our own hand and pat our other arm. Grasp the lesson learned and apply it for forever.

We learn lessons from hurdles only. But if you closely examine even the process of going through difficulty will also appear beautiful to you. Every moment has its own meaning, value and importance. We just need to realise it by looking at it with a higher perspective. The tough the problem is the closer you are going to feel with the almighty, he is going to embrace you along with all your strength and limitations. Hurdles are meant to overcome our limitations and welcome growth with opened arms.

We normally cling on to people we love or things we have expected to last long only because we are afraid of the idea of losing that we keep on trying to hold on to them until the very end when we finally realise that we are only hurting ourselves. We are afraid that we might lose our happiness with that loss but sometimes those are not loss those are actually win because losing everything that brings you pain in one way or another is always a win. As after losing such things or people we actually find peace and purity in our life. That loss is a loss until when you realise your worth and clearly start seeing things that you deserve. And you will start experiencing these things when you will sit alone to vibe alone for a few days. Don't just let yourself go with the flow of the stream as it might prove hazardous at times, learn to pull yourself back before a downstream comes into your life.

As I told you even undergoing the process of hard times can also seem alluring as everything depends on our perspective. Happiness or sadness is only a state of mind and momentary. As these are only states of mind, they don't define our life what defines us is our mental thought processes, our way of appreciating things around us and our opinion about life. We all are different from one another and that difference decides our destiny. Our characteristics leads us counter our fate and those characteristics are also the gifts of God. That's how we are made, built with the elements that will eventually lead us where we were destined to be. Each one of us carry a unique composition of mental processes, abilities, limitations, ideation, emotions, attitudes, motifs etc.

Everything is pre-determined we are here for just the stake of acting our parts and proving our worth to the greater power. So, we are nothing more than actors working as per the instructions of the divine.

So, who are we to wish for a happy ending in our life story we are here to live it, so just leave it man! Don't just sit and wait for a happy ending to come and kiss you with love live each moment of your life to the extreme. Experiencing sorrow? then feel it to the extreme so that next day that sorrow can't threaten you anymore. Experiencing happy moments? then live to the extreme because nobody knows when will be the next time you will be this happy. Just enjoy the very process of life.

Happy endings in real life are not the actual endings those are only ending of a segment of life. Then again comes a new start of another cycle. This is what our life process is. Live your life as one day at a time, yes, it is difficult to do this but we can just try to get up every day with a new desire and enthusiasm to live this day better than yesterday. We can try to live life daily with new hopes of being a bit better person than yesterday. Have faith in yourself, encourage yourself, trust the good person inside you and make that person finer and wiser with every passing day. Don't just sit and regret things accept your mistakes as those were the things that you did when you were you and you will manage to be a better you tomorrow . Promise yourself to bloom like a rose, to shine like a star and become a beautiful person like that of cherry blossoms. Ok so keeping the similes apart grow every day. Growth doesn't come with effort for a day or two you need to maintain consistency as consistency pays harder and healthier. Each day is a new opportunity to grab and consistent efforts can open unexpectedly amazing doors for you. Believe in the process of life the downs are made to make you understand what ups are like, to value the goodness of life.

Chapter 3

Have you ever witnessed the moon while sitting in a green grass field, have you ever stared at it and wondered how nature guides us by providing light both in day time and night time? Have you ever tried to feel how nature takes care of us by being with us in each and every second of the day? How the sun, moon and stars keep accompanying us to each and every part of the world. Come on the universe is always taking your side and what are you waiting for to be happy? The almighty is always keeping an eye on us rewarding us for our good deeds and punishing us for the bad one, this is how divine justice comes in no time. Believe in the power of almighty and just keep on the good work, keeping being the better person no matter what never leave the good path because everything pays at the right time. Trust the divine timing and stay tuned with the positive growth work of every day.

Life is too short to worry about things that haven't happened yet or doesn't have an existence. Life is too short to stick on things that doesn't set your soul on fire. Set yourself free from everything that is holding you back from growth because growth is the only reason why we were sent to earth, FOR GROWTH OF OUR SOUL. Give importance to development at soul level over everything else this is the ultimate aim of every human life. We all are here to learn, acquire and implement knowledge to give a flourishing shape to our lives.

Stop clinging on to things that are not meant to stay in your life allow the universe to take the control of your life and you will actually witness magic in reality. As like Devi

Draupadi in Mahabharat was blessed with an endless saree by Lord Krishna when after trying her best she gave up the complete control of the situation in the hands of the universe her faith and self-control compelled the almighty to help her out. Her soulful prayer brought her silent win in that situation. We think that the endless saree was a magic and yes, it is true, but that was possible because her soul was that aligned with the positive power of the universe. And Lord Krishna was able to do so because his heart and soul was filled with positive power and at that moment, he attracted all the positive vibrations of the universal energies. They together proved that purity in soul, purity in intentions and the never-ending desire to attract positive growth at soul level is everything that makes you a greater human. Devi Draupadi tried her best to help herself in that tragic situation until the very end. I want to tell you here that give your best with pure intentions until the very end and when the end arrives the divine power will be there to hold you from behind, give you a tight hug and appreciate your efforts. So, let's not just wait for happy endings let's live each moment with purity at heart.

Let's prove our worth in every moment of life by finely representing the goodness of thoughts bring manufactured in our mind at present. So, let's start enjoying as for the present phase, keeping the worries of past aside and imagination of future too, living for now.

Believe in goodness of each moment, trust the process of evolution both within you and in your environment because everything happening with you has some meaning which you are going to realise sooner or later. Part by part, little by little you are going to make progress in life. Create your own happiness by living in independent ways and welcoming all positivity at once.

Chapter 4

Happy endings are not everything that we need to look for, we need to look for lessons, values, transformations, changes and moralities. Because these are the things that will help you transform into an excellent individual. If you will start doing this you then can clearly observe how uniquely good and special you are than most of the people. Don't just go with the flow of people around you don't let them influence your mind every time. Stand out once and you are never going to return being that individual who always follows or agrees with other's opinions. Learn to embrace yourself before anyone else. Yes, be a better individual, help others, love others, be there for people but don't ever let yourself down for anybody else. Lessons built our personality, values make us a sympathetic individual, transformation gives a new shape to our lives, change makes us taste different aspects of life and moralities define who we are. So now it is completely your choice about how much importance you want to give to these 5 things. You came to this world with the grace of God and now it is up to you how you want to live it. Whether to live it with values and ethics or just go with the flow. Choices and decisions of our present moment decides our future. Values and ethics will lead you to achieve the best positive fate of your life. Yes, there will be hurdles, there will be difficulties in your way of maintaining your values but just give it a try don't stress much just give an easy try with good intention. Leave the rest on your fate to decide. We are here to play our part not to stress over things those are out of our control. We are here to take the healthiest step every time to yield highest positivity out of everything. Not everything that we come in contact with are meant for us, some are there to teach us a few lessons of life so that in future we can value what God wants us to have. Don't live your life hanging over things like that, learn to let go. Try to understand the secret messages of the almighty with everything that is happening with you.

Start analysing things from multiple dimensions, start looking at things with different perspective to add more ideas to your mind. These dimensions will help you observe even the minute happiness of life. And eventually you will meet your authentic self, one day. Your authentic self is the one who will be carrying all positive traits that you look for in the universe. She[/he] will be the one who will be fearless to achieve the desired goal not harmful but wearing a powerful self, capable enough to protect herself, guide herself on the right path. She[/he] won't be that unpaid maid anymore. She[/he] will be the ruler of her world busy with her progress stuffs, managing everything brilliantly that she was unable to do earlier. Once you find your authentic self, life will be so much easier than you can imagine, the quest is up to that only. Keep examining yourself each and every moment ask yourself what are you expecting and from whom and why? What else could have made you feel soulful? And why can't you do that for yourself? How can you reach that stage of self-satisfaction in everything? Then you can easily find-what you want to be? how you want it to be? Both your authentic self and the path to find that. You don't have to wear a mask of anything that hides the real you, be you and be proud of the goodness you carry with it. The hustle is up to the moment when you realise your true mental peace and actual happiness.

After finding your genuine self you will be capable of differentiating between things and people who are healthy for you and who are dangerous. We need to be very careful while allowing people to enter into our lives, always keep in mind your mental health and well-being are the two most precious things of your life. Don't ever put them aside for anything else, never let anyone exploit them in any way. Cause at the end you will be responsible for what you are going to face. I don't want to scare you but this is a real fact. You are going to appreciate yourself if you allow good people into your life and blame yourself if you did the opposite.

Then why not choose to appreciate yourself every time by embracing positivity and positive people. Then you might be thinking how to identify good ones and bad ones. The most prominent difference is the bad ones are going to agree with your every choice and the good one will stop you in every wrong step as they are leaders of their lives, they are not easy-going people they carry their values and ethics with them. They are the one who will love you unconditionally even if you don't listen to them and keep making wrong choices with bad people, they will always be standing at a corner celebrating your mini successes and will give you a healing hug after you realise them as the best person of your life. My eyes are moist while writing this because I actually have such gems in my life and I feel so fortunate having them. Once you find them don't ever lose them keep them till eternity. They are the true diamonds of this world. Surround yourself with those people who reflect what you want to be because energies are contagious.

Once you install all positive people and allow all positive vibrations of this universe to come to you there will be nothing impossible for you, there can be no heights of the world that you can't reach. You will be a free soul with angelic wings to explore every magical thing of this world. Just have faith in the power of universe and keep moving towards positivity. No matter how tough times get, find gratitude knowing that times will always get better, if you are carrying positivity within you nothing can stop you from witnessing divine light.

Find your light, find your true self and own it with grace.

Priorities your daily growth over everything and start walking on the path of goodness and light.

Here we conclude there is no need to search for happy endings each moment is made to be lived with purity at heart and goodness in mind. Every day is meant to experience certain aspects or emotions of human life. So, let's extract the best positive lessons out of every seconds of this life. Be the best version of yourself and your life will grow way faster than you can ever imagine. Listen to your soul before taking decisions in anything, it is your best guide on earth. Let your soul and mind work in collaboration with each other. Before allowing anyone to come into your life pay some attention to the voice of your soul if it feels ok to do that. Take time in everything, be slow but steady, be gentle to yourself, don't carry the burden of other's expectations on your shoulder.

We suffer, we struggle, we survive
then magic arrives and magic stays.

CHAPTER THREE

WHY DO WE EXPECT HAPPINESS FROM OTHERS?

Chapter 1

Exchange of happiness between our family members and friends are the things that we mostly rely on to be happy. On a general note, we wait on our special days like birthday or anniversary or any festive days like Holi, Diwali etc. for our special ones to come to us with amazing surprises and brighten up our day with extra love and nourishment. We all do that actually we all keep expecting certain things from certain people because we think our happiness depends on the way they treat us.

Not only for happiness generally our moods depend on how others treat us. We rely on things that are happening to us on a particular day to consider it as a good day or a bad day. It is very fair to exchange opportunities of creating happiness for one another. More straight forwardly we mostly rely on our surrounding individuals and environment to choose our state of mind.

We feel more cheerful in a gathering with friends or family than when alone. We are humans, we are social animals we need people to talk to, to converse with, to share and create our memories; that's what keeps us alive and going.

But have you ever been through a day when you are feeling being drained by life and you are looking for someone to shower some sustaining love on you but somehow you haven't found anyone of that kind and now you are clueless about what you want to do to get through this? We all to go through certain days like this. Those days are meant to teach us how to cheer ourselves up.

Have you ever been on a walk with your-self?

I mean to say just a walk with your true self, the real person, the real you. Not trying to force yourself to smile or act in any other way that you don't need to do due to presence of another person. Not trying to be someone who you are not or don't want to be, in that particular moment. A walk without an aim to reach to. Talking to yourself without uttering so many words just muttering in fragments, remembering your foolish side and giving a brief smirk on it, smiling at your old self, admiring your new self with much more love and honesty. Just loving yourself a bit more with every passing smirk, smile, laughter all together with every passing moment. Simply walking with a never-ending desire to make yourself better, provide yourself better warmth and the desire of being more devoted to your soul.

And then returning home with a bag full of promises such as spending more time to take your care by doing stuffs to make your skin glow, body to feel fresh and active; conversing more with yourself; buying a small gift for you every day like a cup of cappuccino, a mouse cake, a pastry, a fancy umbrella or a fancy purse. Promising to harness your energy at positive things only. Promising to treat your loved ones better even when in high temper so as to be a good human in real as words told in agony hits hard the most so just cut it out. Promising to hold your other hand and stop being anyone else's unpaid maid, carrying all your power with smoothness and gentility. The promise to feel the love of the universe for you every now and then and never ever to feel discouraged at any moment even if when you are feeling down on some days just to face the mood swing with braveness and then come back to feel the magical life once again. Add or create things that will build on immense pleasure in your daily routine like listening to your favourite songs, your favourite artist, doing some crazy art work, having fun every day and don't ever think like I should not be this happy because happiness itself is uncountable so just feel it limitlessly. Promise to create a vogue personality of your own. Promising things like smiling everyday a bit more, taking rest on time, taking meals on time, not trying to impress anyone by pretending, admiring your authentic uniqueness day by day and little by l

Chapter 2

We need to learn how to keep us happy even in distress as that is always our silent win card. Buying yourself chocolates, ice-cream or some soft drinks on a hot summer day, hot coffee in a winter evening might seem really insignificant to some of us but those are the things that will contribute to keep you away from evil thoughts and will motivate you to keep on the hard work & keep going in the right path.

Let's learn to show gratitude to ourself for what we have transformed into today, let's rejoice everything that we have made through until this day. Let's live once again but this time with greater objective and abundant self-love. Gratitude is a super power; it is like the piggy bank of our blessings given by the universe. Let's try to find out reasons in everything to show our gratitude towards the universe as then we will be blessed with more than what we asked for. Let's feel the blessings and feel the power of within in us

Learn to congratulate yourself for every small and big achievements not only in terms of prizes but things that once you were not sure how to do and somehow you have made it successfully. For example, in your school days you might have been through an exam where you were stuck in a question, you were unable to find out the correct answer and you decided to redo it after completing all other questions and at the end when you did it again and you successfully did it correctly. That's an achievement, in fact, a remarkable achievement you managed the tension in between that question and the others, you are a capable person, you proved it.

We need to stop considering ourself insignificant the weight of our words is equally impactful as that of others, the things that we do, the way we do describes the magic that we carry within us. We need to be responsible enough to finely display that magic and for that self-control, self-love and confidence in our self are to be taken into account all-together. As on some days we do somethings knowingly or unknowingly that creates a smile in the face of other people and later they will remind those moments there then they will keep smiling at the same thing over and over again. So, let's fill ourselves up with positivity and lend it to people out there having none of it, let's radiate it in our surrounding through our words and activities.

We all go through difficult phases of life in fact we all are more habituated with difficulties than happiness. Here I want to talk about those major hardships that wreak us down to the level of our soul, when the escape route seems hazy or sometimes just dark. Those nightmares are the things that we are most afraid of things that we always wanted to stay away from, those that we never wanted to come in encounter with. While going through things like sit alone at a peaceful place for some time let your feelings flow whichever way it chooses to, in the meantime try patting one of your shoulder with your other hand and say- "______ [your name] I know you are good human, I know you are good that's it you don't need anyone's opinion to learn who you are, you understand yourself the most. I believe in you and no good person deserves a bad ending. If things haven't taken the right turn yet then it is not the end. Keep up your faith. One day this will end and a new beginning will embrace me."

And then feel your inner strength, feel how powerful you are. We are carrying tremendous power in our soul that constitute to be 0.0000000000000001 per cent of the power of the universe. We are all little mewing and puking babies in the loving arms of the universe keep feeling its immense love now and again. The words that you said to your self will enhance your spiritual capability to face whatever obstacles you have in your path, to face everything in a better and smatter way. Face it for now and live like a warrior for the rest of your life.

God has gifted us the world's most beautiful present that is our life. The way we feel, we sense, we breath, we move everything we do and our soul existence is a magical gift to be cherished. We are ought to give our best, live life to the fullest and enjoy each day as a whole new blessing.

Ups and downs are parts of our life, they combinedly make our life interesting, give us both hope and despair, happy and sad moments. Without despair hope has no value, without sadness there can be no happy moments. hence let's start admire everything, every moment, everyone as they are and most importantly as we are.

Chapter 3

As this book is based on a dialogue from Mrs Warren's Profession written by George Bernard Shaw from those mentioned lines in page 3, we can learn that whatever we are dealing with any circumstances, people, conflicts or whatever it may be, somehow, we are quite responsible for it, our personality automatically attracts things of similar or exactly opposite kinds. We may not feel it or recognize them until we repeatedly go through alike things.

Our persona, perspective and postulations attract similar energies from the universe and put them right into our lives. By now you might have realised that the accelerator and break of your life is in your hands only. We just have to learn driving as a smooth driver does, we need to drive our life with that smoothness and stability. We need to become a licensed driver only. We need to maintain the smooth path of life by choosing peace and stability over everything else.

Hence let's take life in a positive way and let's start designing our own happiness, let's try to find it in everything whether small or big, minute or imaginary, critical or easy, let's find it out anyway let's give it a big hit. We need to enable our self to be happy with everything, it doesn't mean to adjust with things that doesn't appeal us, it means not to accept things but to add things that will provide us pleasure and force us to feel cheerful irrespective of our mood. Back then we were searching for happiness and now let's put a full stop on it and focus on creating our world of joy, by adding new activities or objects that makes us feel lifted every time in a new manner.

Our perspective is the sole reason behind the way we live our life. The way we see things or assume them to be controls the flow of our life. If our vision of life is positive then we can unknowingly overcome many hurdles of life. And if it is negative, we see or assume every minute thing as a hurdle in our path. Hence majority of difficulties that we face are result of our vision and interpretation within us. Most of our problems doesn't even have an existence other than being there in our mind. We usually suffer because of our thoughts on some particular thing those thoughts don't even have a physical existence, it only exists in a pseudo world of assumption.

To stay away from all these pseudo assumptions, we need to focus on the better side of life more. We need to align our life in a way that will lead us on the path of light, away from all those shadowy and hazy part of the world. In order to align in such a way first we should learn to give more attention on the positive signs provided by the universe to us, for example our life style. Secondly, we need to accept all shades of our personality with love and warmth in heart as all of that combinedly makes what we are. Thirdly we should make the habit of meeting our updated version every other day so as to make this world a better place to live in farther away from conflicts and crimes, a place filled with hunger of self-growth, prosperity, love and harmony. When we will start to keep ourselves happy our cheerful mind and light heart will contribute in making the world a happy jolly land. Even the image of this land in my imagination is creating butterflies in my stomach. Hope one day we will actually get to witness something like this, an atmosphere filled with only positive spirit.

Let's begin to stay away from things that make us feel sad or they do not ignite any positive vibration within us. Selfcare is so much more than just promises, or bubble bath or face scrub it includes filling up of our life with individuals who are going to fire up our desire to run in the right path of progress and growth. Those people are going to shake up our foundation hard and re-establish it in an outstanding one. Let's start looking out for people having sprinkle of divinity to add them up in our lives. Let's suffuse our lives with ample positivity.

Find out that particular thing or things that excite you up to your highest euphoric level and hold on to it until eternity. Run towards your euphoria and advancement and say a warm-hearted goodbye to everything that disappoints you. Be unstoppable in the path of including list of happy items.

Finding our true happiness is the first step towards the beginning of a prosperous life as a happy mind gives the more productive and creative output in everything. Hence by being in good mood you are making your life easy and simultaneously contributing your productivity to the society.

Chapter 4

Many of us go through anxiety or depression for those individuals I would like to suggest that whatever is making you go through this you are far more powerful that it. You guys are not abnormal you guys are absolutely normal. Most of us experience these stages of life we all go through similar traumas and setbacks of life but of different versions, there is nothing there to panic about. You people are living examples of what a warrior looks like. See you have or are going through so much and still you are going through my novel, see how stable and capable your mind is, your mind was never a weak one, in fact, it was one of the strongest and is now also, may be that's the reason that the almighty considered you capable of facing all that. Don't consider yourself responsible or blame yourself for anything because at every point you did what the divine power wanted you to do, you were never so wrong and never going to be. We all know the brightest phase of life comes after we pass all dark and scary nights. Your dazzling days are waiting there at the other end of the lane to welcome you with enormous contentment and peace. And then you will realise it was all worth suffering for. Our words and actions echo out in the universe. It is like a ripple effect that will find its way back to us. Whenever you are facing depression or anxiety, I would say let is pass through you don't divert your mind, let it slide out so that you don't have to run away from it every time, tell them "yes I see you coming and I am not afraid of you anymore because you have no existence and I am far more powerful that this shitty feeling." At moments like this look out for the most immediate things that remind you that you are special, you are being loved by so many people out there & you mean a whole lot to them. You are important, you matter and everything you are going through is taking you closer and closer towards your destined happiness. It will take a while hang in there for some time. As the amount of suffering that we are meant to go through is fixed, we just need to let that energy flow through so as to set ourselves free from them one day. Just let it flow. By diverting our mind while facing them we are saving them up for our future, we should not do that, face it and clear it out from your life.

One day while I was on my way back to home after my scheduled morning walk, that day, I was feeling a little tired and was experiencing a bit of pain in my legs, there was only about half a kilometre left to reach my home [my destiny] then I gave a look back and saw how far I have walked down, how far I have made it. In virtue of which the path ahead seemed too small to worry about. I had an option to sit on the street side bench for some time but I chose to walk and reach my destination on time. There is always an option available for us to cover the whole path in one go or going at our own pace to reach out to our destiny. I am not asking you to keep walking like me to reach there on time I am explaining the concept of path of life and asking you to choose your option. Take your time if you want to or be on time or if you want to take it slowly regardless of the way you will choose to go one day you will make it, that is what matters the most you made it at the end.

See whatever we are going through is ultimately creating the pathway to our sparkling future. Let's trust our path to end at somewhere like a blue sea beach with a number of fire flies as in Virginia Beach giving the assurance of brand new shining fresh start. Keep that spirit up in you even while facing the worst adversities of life and one day you will get there, we all will.

Try taking yourself on a date with yourself as love increases as we spend time with our loved ones similarly our self-growth flourishes as we spend more time with us. Try watching your best-loved movie with in your happy with your favourite snacks, be seated at your best comfortable posture on the bed. Try finding happiness in cleaning your home with your mother and witness her eyes filled with proudness. Try finding satisfaction in filling up of all the empty bottles of the house. Take the feeling of a Bollywood heroine while spreading up the wet clothes at the terrace. Try feeling like a high-profile employee while working on your office tasks, experience the pride of being you. Find happiness in realising how beautifully you have evolved into a responsible individual.

Take a short break for some time while feeling low, enjoy hardest in each single moment of that tiny break. Everything is preparing us for better opportunities, for more better days. It is creating a more mature and powerful us. It is preparing us to deal with further difficulties of life. These are building up our personality that we need to complete our mission on earth for which we were born. All that twist and turns have their own meaning that we will realise at different points of life. The direction that we are going to choose to get out of troubles will define who are in future. Hence let's be wise and cool while dealing with lemon punches of life. In due course of time, we will realise that the worst thing that happened to us was the best thing that could happen for us.

Chapter 5

There will be days where we will experience being empty, lonely and helpless, on days like his we won't be able to express our feelings clearly to someone as it is just emptiness. These emptiness and loneliness are creating space for future happiness those are about to enter into our lives in a matter of few months hang in there for some time.

Stop waiting for people to provide you pleasure or happiness. Start learning yourself better, start holding yourself better, start getting closer to yourself. Look out for what excites you the best, find out what sets fire in your soul, run for it, walk for it, crawl for it but just don't let it go for free even without trying. As distress brings out the best version of us onto the surface and the darkest night comes with the brightest day in flip.

It is quite easy to get reminded about looking after our physical health as our body keeps on giving us signals of what we are in need of. But the signs of spiritual needs are not as apparent as that of the physical. We may feel sad, dull and uninspired but we don't realise it is our spirit that needs care. Our spiritual health is directly proportional to the connection we feel to the world around us. Open your heart to feel the love and grace of the divine and uplift your spirits. Spend time saying your prayers and give yourself space to listen to for answers. Your inner wisdom is how the divine speaks to you. Ensure that you have time to listen to your inner wisdom to make sure to understand what it wants you to know. Spend time in solitude to collect your thoughts and find inner happiness and peace.

Begin to explore what allows you experience the true aura of life, go for a long solo journey to any other state or country and feel the substitution of large variety of feelings, get lost in the snowy hills or desserts or open flower fields for the time being and experience what being solo and carefree feels like to be. Give yourself time to realise how your heart and mind work in collaboration, how they work in synchronisation to let you have the best out of everything. Start doing things that will let you overcome your weaknesses, do that after preparing yourself, after taking sufficient time to make up your mind ready to face it anyway. Because a man with weaknesses can reach only a certain height, he can't witness the world beyond that horizon. Start clearing your weaknesses and limitations one by one at you own speed to experience the true magic of this flawless universe. Don't settle for less, don't adjust if you are capable enough of breaking out. I am not asking you to start a revolt or something negative like that I am just asking you to look out for more peaceful and positive ways to enhance your life the way you want it to be, work for it instead of just being sad and demotivated start taking small steps towards your dreams and goals.

Few more instantaneous and affordable ways of lifting your moods are as such- buying some scrapbooks or colour papers to do all that funny stuffs on them like collecting natural things and pasting them in mini bags or writing some crazy things about everyone around you, drawing their ugly pictures; buy few sheets of drawing papers, pull out your painting colours and just draw some random meaningless stuffs on them and then give a big naughty and satisfied smile by looking at it. For a bit insane way play that happy go lucky songs of your playlist and dance like shit according to the tune, try matching with the steps of original video and laugh hard at your wrong steps. The more you choose to focus on the lighter side of the life, the easier it will be for you to get through the so-called turbulence. Happiness is best experienced by keeping our inner child alive. Bring it out for enjoying the simple pleasures of life. What can't be fought through boldness can be fought through cuteness, use this phrase to set yourself free from traumas of depression, rough experiences etc. Be a bit flexible and easy on yourself while dealing with things that affect your mental health as you are the only person who is able to understand clearly what you are encountering with.

Go easy go slow, your physical and mental health both are equally important. Happiness is worthy when we are physically and mentally fit. Choose to look at the lighter side of the life, taste the joy of simplicity and subtle innocence. Keep adding minute stuffs that will continue to add delight in you. Allow the cold breeze to play with your precious shiny hair. Continue or start smiling at little things, let your heart flutter around within its healthy perimeter, let your exquisite mind acquire transcendent peace.

Self-care will fabricate true ecstasy within us.

CHAPTER FOUR

WHY DO WE BLAME CIRCUMSTANCES?

Chapter 1

Circumstances are the universe's way of unfolding things with which we were meant to cross our paths with. The way things unfold for us from time to time are different. For example, when we were at the age of early-childhood we had to follow the instructions of elders every time and as we grew up with growing age and education, we developed the ability to be our own guide and elders too started to give us space of putting our point of view, our opinions got the chance of being heard. As time passes, situations change accordingly, sometimes they turn favourable while at other they turn unexpectedly bad. Dealing with good circumstances is a matter of kid stuff, so what defines us is how we deal with adverse situations.

The manner in which we accept situations in our mind directly formulates our life.

Once or more we all have played the blame game at some points of our lives, we blame circumstances, people, ourselves and the most common and easy to blame-the almighty. But does this help us to improve our life in any way? No, right? We are made with such components and power of nature that enable us to look out for our desired situations and if we aren't able to find it, we create them [the dialogue on which this book is based on] we get up every day to search new ways to approach life we realise it or not we do. Our desires, our expectations, our wishes keep on changing every day, our outlook on life last year is not the same this year. This change is gradual and progressive.

We have learned about Newton's first law of motion that, if a body is at rest or moving at a constant speed in a straight line, it will remain at rest or keep moving in a straight line at same speed unless and until it is acted upon by a force.

We can apply this in our life too.

First have a view over what the pamphlet of what your life looks like and if you are happy with it or are willing for a change in it. We have to be organised with everything that we do, calculation is much needed to keep going in the best path available to go in every junction. We need to keep checking on our life in a particular interval, where we are moving to and this path is leading us to what.

If after having a thorough look you feel like things are not at proper place then give that external force whether to kick out certain things or to bring in some. And if you feel like things are good to go with then just take a sweet rest for a while and let things fall into proper place.

Think about a big white hall with several windows, doors and screens, those are moving heavily due to strong breeze and some lighter things of the room are flying here and there. As you enter the room what will be your first move? You need to close the doors and windows and keep the things back into place if you want them to be in order again and if not then you will just leave it as it is. Sometimes when things are getting out of hands or not giving a soothing texture to life then editing is much required. Take the responsibility of your life in your own hands. Stop relying, stop looking out for help stand up like a lioness, as she is someone who rules over the ruler [the lion].

Chapter 2

There are basically two types of energies in the practical world of living being, those are outer energy and inner energy. Outer energy is the one which keeps influencing our lives by being an external force that we call as circumstances or situations. Mostly they try to bend our lives the way we don't want to and at other times they turn on our life in an unexpectedly amazing way. We need to sense things or situations before they take a major turn, we need to stay closer to the signs given to us by our spirit guides or you can say guardian angels. You might have marked how people of different countries are surrounded with different animals and how that feels obvious to us in our day-to-day life, god has kept us surrounded with a number of heavenly energies revolving around us as part of nature that feels very normal to us. In India we are surrounded by dogs, cows, bulls etc while people of Australia are surrounded by kangaroo, platypus, echidna etc. Those spirit guides convey us signals through animals, birds, repeating numbers or lucky numbers and many more things those are unexpectedly expected for us. They try to hint us if that particular day will turn out to be good or bad. I am not talking about blind beliefs here, I am trying to make you aware of what you are surrounded with, what you personally feel and experience in daily life. I want you to feel the way your spirit guide or guides are trying to help you out. If we stay in tune with shifts of energies around us, we can easily overcome difficulties and manifest opportunities. Put emphasis on how things turn for you and you will be able to get a higher perspective of your life.

The other one is inner energy, that I have mentioned earlier, the way we carry ourselves in both adverse and favourable circumstances, we naturally mature with age, our character gets refined as we grow old and see consequences of our actions. It includes our mental processes, our beliefs, our upbringing, our ideas and the limit that we set in our mind for the way we need to live it.

We can't control outer energy we can only make our assumptions based on our observations made by looking at the things that keeps on happening with us in a casually rare way. We can only control our inner energy rooted within our heart and mind. The better we connect with our inner self the less impact we will experience by the outer energy. Have you seen renowned actors or performers performing on a grand stage with hundreds of audiences, how they do that with a smile on their face and not exhibiting even a single drop of nervousness in it? The more renowned and famous the actor is the more deeply he/she is connected with 'the self'. They perform at stage when all lights are focused on them, they do it so easily that the viewer will feel it as easy as like that of eating a piece of cake. Have you ever given a thought about how a few actors of any movie industry come up with blockbuster movie every year? It has many reasons one of them is that particular actor is so much well acquainted with his/her self that every time while choosing a movie he/she best examines if that fits in with his real character or not; or he/she can come up with a character that best fits the movie or not. This proves that whatever the circumstances may be how hard, how breath taking, we have the inbuilt ability in us to breakthrough every single negative energy, we just need to connect with that energy within us. The actors while performing they don't focus on what is in front of them whether that large audience or that lights and camera, they are just portraying their self, they are immerged with what's within them, what they have learned, what their training and experiences instructs them and not what surrounds them. The hard work they do to come in front of camera involves connecting with their self and finding the true talent that their spirit carries in this lifetime. When people see an actor giving an outstanding performance, they say that particular actor went into the character so well, but the true fact is he/she has brought out that character from within 'the self', he/she brought it out from his/her core and showed it to the audience in a fantastic way. Because it was brought out from the core the actor didn't felt any difficulty while acting like that rather he/she felt the ease of showing what's there within him/her. As the character itself doesn't have an existence [keeping exceptions aside], the actor is the one who brings the character to life by allowing it to shine from within.

We all have thousands of shades of our personality that we carry within us, we are not quite known to every shade, we cross our paths with new and amazingly modified versions of us under certain circumstances that compel our higher self to put that shade into play. Let's try to examine how we react, how we arrange words every time we converse, how we converse with different people under different circumstances. Let's sit in front of the mirror one day and look at our 'self' and adore a few versions of the self, let's try to feel a few shades each day for our sake only. Let's embrace and cherish each shade with love and affection as we grow.

Chapter 3

If universe is a huge bird, then, each day of our life with certain number of situations in it, that bird will continue to shade its feathers one by one to keep us safe and happy in every single circumstance. That bird will continue to protect us until when it loses all its feathers with a deep affection in its heart that it has stored for us. In other words, we call it as our angle.

Remember even the bleakest and bitter days carry the tiny spark of the magic that you are meant to witness in future. We only need to keep our eyes and ears wide open for the signs of heaven.

And from the moment you will start counting on yourself as your starlight, no individual or no form of outer energy will be able to push you into darkness.

Normally we people use a phrase 'what the hell' in our common spoken English language for things that irritate us. Our use of words, their arrangement, the way we speak our tone, our pitch define our personality and simultaneously bring in similar energies of the universe in terms of people, circumstances and situations. While we use such phrases with negative terms in them like the word 'hell', we don't realise what price we are paying for using such words. One way or other way around we pay for such negative terms through the difficulties that we face. Repeated use of these kinds of words acts as additional sheets of the real exam paper of difficulty. Let's learn the act of management of words in order to start attracting positive universal energies that will help us get through tough things more easily than before. Let's promise to never use such words like hell for anything no matter how stressful it is, let's be thoughtful every time.

We people who are sociable, we think, that we can go good with everyone by being good to all. There is no harm to be good to all. Your intentions are good but no one can guarantee how situations will turn out. And we all need to fix this in our mind that at every phase of life we are led by one particular kind of energy. It is upon us either to allow anybody else's energy to lead us or just only our own aura. Most of the time we unknowingly get influenced by a single person's aura and that's the moment we need to check and stop it if it is suffocating or not letting us to go in a balanced way. No other energy should take the lead of the path of your life other than yours, let them come and go with ease and keep yours fixed. Don't let the influence of thoughts or words of anyone completely fill up your mind. Our mind is like that of a bowl of maggi, it can contain only one pack of it, we have to choose wisely on what particular idea we should rely our life to be.

Like the use of popular phrases, we do so many things just because we see other people doing that, we also have influencers around us in social medias. I don't understand why people need influencers? Aren't we capable enough to build our own uniquely special identity and keep ourselves influenced by our own distinct ideas?

We need to start taking lead of our own life, we need to start being our own influencer. Before taking any decisions may it be minute or big rethink if it suits your personality, if it defines you well as a good person, if it is helping you to move upward in life.

Each circumstance that we come across are like those scratch codes of life, we need to scratch the messages of lessons and add it to our list of ideas upon which our life dwells. They are here to make sure we are evolving.

Feeling of stability in synchronisation of our emotions by listening to our mind, body and soul will help us eradicate lots and lots of negativity in terms of people, their words, their actions, their way of treating us and everything else that was able to affect us earlier.

At many circumstances we just suffer because we are not trying to look out of the box and navigate through so many possible ways that can swiftly take us out of it, into a smoother world. Being easy on yourself and a bit of calmness in most of the circumstances can bring out magical results, if we start to believe in it.

Chapter 4

If we set an aim to choose peace of mind over anything else, then honey, nothing can make you wipe your tears until you allow them to affect you. Make an entrance gate for everything and keep your security guard[mind] there to check things and allow only and only good and best things to enter your life. You might not be able to realise the importance of this security check now. As we realise the value and goodness of getting a nap in a non-scheduled time after witnessing a storm in life where we didn't get to sleep for countless nights by just weeping and begging to get through it desperately. Whatever may be the circumstances priorities a heathy peaceful state of mind every single time, it might not reward you with instant magical gifts but with the course of time, it will, definitely.

Yes, sometimes circumstances may turn drastically negative in an unexpected way. What to do then? Many people have many different answers to this particular question each one varies from one another. But the fact is we will keep searching for answers to this same question every time until we find out, what is exactly wrong within us? Until we find that and rectify it universe will keep throwing the same kind of balls over and over again from different angles only. Sometimes we see ourselves as the ultimate sufferer or the victim of the situation, no that's not the solution. Yes, we might be the sufferer, we might be someone who had only good intention, and still, we need to learn one more chapter. To quickly identify what's exactly wrong within us every time we need to stay tuned to our heart and soul in every single moment of life, as they are going to make us aware which path to choose and when to choose. There are certain circumstances which we can't avoid repeatedly they keep following us until we encounter them boldly. Let's accept them as compulsory subjects of life. But trying every day to stay connected with our 'self'.

But there will also be circumstances which are going to fill our heart with tremendous love and happiness. This time we will be so busy enjoying them that soulful connection with the self will be kept aside for a few days. Ok dear, enjoy as much as you want, we get what we deserve, so ultimately you have earned it anyway. Let it fill you mind with feeling of living in paradise. But then there the soul will be like, "hey! how can you not take me to your journey to paradise," we actually take it with us but many a times we don't feel that connection because we haven't paid attention to it. Try paying attention to it once and you will experience your happiness increasing into ten folds than earlier.

Our soul is like our mother and father both. It will love us unconditionally, will care for us again unconditionally like our mothers do. And it will also save us from adverse situations, will teach us greater lessons of life like our fathers do. It is closely connected with the magical realm of the universe; it is so much more powerful than with what we can relate. Let it guide you completely in the path of life, trust its instructions doubtlessly.

Now you might me wandering how to connect with your soul so deeply. If you are wandering then here are some ways to try, meditate- this simple one word of 8 letters holds the power to transform the life of every human being; stay alone- by choosing to stay alone for some time and letting your thoughts flow in wherever direction they want to, you are going to find your soul one day after traveling this unknown & unnamed path for certain number days. Imagine your look alike soul standing in a dense green forest with a flowing stream and dazzling sunlight spreading all over the forest, waiting at your side of the stream and you have reached there after a lot of hustle and bustle, it was waiting there for you since years. Now you are finally hugging it and saying "Hey beauty, I got you, my solution for everything is right in front of my eyes now, I love you, thank you for waiting for me here all alone for so long years & I am sorry for being so late." now wipe those teary eyes and give a flying kiss to your heart [who keeps you alive] for letting you witness this day, even if it is just textual now you can make it real one day.

By now you might have realised how peaceful it is to spend some quality time alone or with your instant family, away from negative people, away from social media and those so- called influencers out there.

Chapter 5

Circumstances are only the visual representation of qualities of all people in that particular room. Or we can say the circumstances that cover our life path are visual representation of our personality only. So, whatever may be the circumstances in the outside world we always need to keep a private room for ourself in our mind available to keep the balance of our thoughts and actions in line and length.

Our soul is in the journey to gain a human life experience on earth, that's it. Don't hang over things which are proving to be hard on you, don't tolerate any kind of burden on your soul. You are here to live and enjoy the taste of life on earth just focus on that. Circumstances will change with time, good and bad situations combinedly contribute on our journey of life. Keep that higher perspective, of journey of human life on earth, on every time, and not letting these tiny minute circumstances which have the life span of a few days upset you in any possible manner. We need to keep going, we know that, but I am here asking to do it with a soulful smile on your face, not upset over anything, not happy over any materialistic thing, not hanging over the people you wanted to be with you and many more earthly things, just truly and genuinely happy with who you are and your pace of self-growth. This sense of soulful happiness will create a sense of completeness and peace within you. You won't be then looking out for reasons to smile or things to give pleasure to your eyes, life will seem complete even when you are alone and so much smoother and softer than before. This will keep you at a distance from earthly happiness, and will take you closer to the universal one. Life will become effortlessly peaceful from all directions as you are no longer clinging on to anything. Let's be honest with our soul, our ability, our capability, our strength, our weaknesses and everything else that we have as gifts of god. Let's honestly and wisely start being true to our roots and origin by accepting them confidently. Let's prove that we are so much more powerful than these tiny earthly circumstances, as we have 3 great gadgets- heart, mind and soul, gifted to us by the divine power to have a cool and sparkling experience of life on earth.

Even if the universe has the key of our life in its hands which controls and decides the circumstances that we witness, we still have the lock with us, the power to decide if they can leave a good impact or bad impact on us. There is always a bit of possibility in our hands to turn things the way we can choose to have, the least negative impact and allow to learn and accept the positivity it had on its other side. Our humanitarian process of evolving into an excellent individual requires certain degree of difficulties, certain situations, facing of few individuals, hard circumstances etc. so that we can acquire priceless human personalities as like the case of diamonds. Diamond itself has no light but we keep on phrasing, to shine like a diamond, because it absorbs light when exposed to it and reflects it in the darkness, we have to do the same, we need to attract positivity, that is light in case of diamond, and have to reflect it when circumstances drag us into darkness. That is how we can become our own starlight.

Staying composed and alert to how situations evolve in front of us and having a deep sense on how to react will set us as an example in the society as what the personality of a responsible and fully awakened person seems like. Every situation provides us ample options on how to react to them, let's rethink, let's choose what best fits to our personality at that particular time and place.

We see circumstances through the glass of our mind let's wipe it often as we do to our specks.

Connect truly with your roots to determine what suits you well.

CHAPTER FIVE

WHY AREN'T WE ABLE TO FIND REAL FREEDOM?

Chapter 1

Being humans we all have the desire to experience that carefree and euphoric kind of freedom at certain moments of our life. We all wish to witness that amazing fascination that the word freedom creates within us. We people of 21st century have those bucket list kinds of things which includes foreign trips, long bike rides, attending concerts of our favourite idols, being on a solo trip and many more that we aim to fulfil as parts of our entire idea of freedom.

On an honest note, fascination, dreams & desires all together constitutes our idea of freedom. We see freedom as something that sets us free from the so-called rules of a family, society or a community. We see it as a new and fancy way of living human life in actual world. It is a common idea of tasting all unique pleasures available on earth by nature or by new and advanced technologies.

The question is from where did we learn this? who taught us that freedom is that fancy thing that we acquire after struggling our own bit?

Actually, we all have different definition of freedom depending on our phase of life, our experiences, our ideas of living, our beliefs all together play a great role in determining what freedom should be like for us. Our picturization of freedom may vary from person to person but the basic idea joined with it since the beginning is our ultimate happiness.

Now what I am going to share, you might think that these are ideas that look well and fine in texts and essays not in reality, well, that completely depends on your perspective, I will just try to make you feel how easy it is to experience a few shades of real freedom in life.

First let's examine the word 'FREEDOM' can you see it has a word- 'FREE' attached to it, we all know what free means. Here I want you to have a look on things that are free for us since birth our body, our mental health, our physical health, our soul, our beloved family & our forever evergreen [with love] school friends. We never asked anyone before birth to bless us with such priceless gifts of the world, those were given to us as signs of love and blessings by the realms of universe before entering into the life of human being.

Before longing or wishing to have those fancy experiences of freedom let's think, shouldn't we look after these blessings more and take care of them every day. Our idea of fancy freedom will turn worthless if we lose even a single free blessing that we have. A beautiful trip to one amazing place will seem worthless if our mental health is not so ok. We won't be able to do those crazy and funny things that we had wished to do once we reach our dream destination if our physical health is not good. We won't be able to experience that extreme level of happiness if one of our funny friend or family member haven't joined us in the trip. We won't be able to really enjoy that funky party with a few fake friends out there.

We should learn to value those free gifts of nature before asking for more, we need to embrace and cherish things that prove dear to us and add the spirit of magic in our lives. We need to pay heed to those gifts that are always present with us to remind us how special we are.

We realise the worth of normalcy after going through a mental, physical or emotional rough stage. Rather than running after and searching here and there for happiness and freedom that we learn by looking at other's wonderful ideas, focusing on the goodness of our life will lead us to witness a healthy lifestyle. Healthy lifestyle is the one that focus on our good mental and physical health. When we focus more on maintaining good heathy lifestyle, we need to set ourselves free from stressing our mind to get that dreamy life without preparing it to go through similar range of difficulties.

The pleasure of standing at the balcony in a cold evening with a warm cup of coffee, after working hard for weeks is one of those ultimate freedom of a human life as that is how we realise how capable we are that we worked hard for so many days, we realise our productivity after working this hard only. Taking a moment and appreciating our efforts in every field of life not only the work field will make us realise how beautiful is our soul, mind and heart and more over our 'self'. Yes, parties may help you to release the stress but this will make you love yourself more, appreciate your worth & know yourself better. A bit of selfcare and self-nourishment through such small measures are always an outstanding idea of loving the soft flow of life.

Chapter 2

We all wish to achieve something great in life and sometimes that's what makes us keep going while at other times it makes us feel low and useless, instead of motivating us, it sometimes turns into stress.

Let's discuss about the stress factor why we face it? It comes to us when we witness or think that the situation in which we are in is far more powerful or impactful than our potential to handle it. Before taking the stress, ask yourself- do you have the clear idea of what is your actual potential? If yes, then have a happy stressful day or face it hard with your true spirit. And if no, take time to determine your worth, your potential your overall net worth of this life. Here take time means to have a look or test yourself to determine your extreme level of capability. We need to find out what best fits us in every way not just the go with the flow thing rather I was made for this thing. This will gift us freedom for the rest of our life on earth. Things that we are good or best at is that ultimate freedom that will keep us away from any kind of mental stress related to work.

Whatever we are working at now or will be working in future whatever it maybe it should be done with a cool mind with a perfect blend with presence of mind, we all know work done with a fresh and cool mind enhances the quality of the work to the extreme. Here also we need to use that coolness to take time and think with a fresh mind from where to start at.

The time to determine the actual field that will give us a free life depends on our pace of understanding- who am I? what activity brings a cheerful smile on my face? In which field I can excel the most? We all have a special feature inbuilt in us we just need to thoroughly have a look at ourselves. We all are different from one another in so many ways, some of us are very clear about their own talents from the very beginning and rest others, we take our time to find out exactly what best fits us.

Have you ever experienced a moment or a few moments in life when your heart or soul or mind, any one of them or just all of them is/are shouting like-this is it/I am loving it!

Those are the moments we actually live for. Life brings those moments to us in unique ways, new and fantastic each time. Here imagine you being the reason of your own feeling of this kind. The idea itself brings such tremendous feeling of happiness and freedom at their best. To make ourselves the reason behind our happiness, first we have to reduce the distance between me and my soul, when we will start moving close and closer to ourselves, we will move farther and farther from the problems that surrounds us.

We all wish to live every day of our life full of blessings of love, happiness and freedom. We keep trying to search for our treasure box, of happiness and true freedom, in so many things like in different places, people, things, dresses, ornaments, situations, books, writings, materialistic things and many other scopes of it. And we all are greedy enough to long for all of it, that's human nature and that's our birth right too.

I would say stop looking for freedom in the outside world it's already within you.

Freedom is not something that we gain after having a bit of argument with our family or relatives or the society. It is something that bounds our soul to shout it out loudly that – This is so peaceful! This is my home! This is what I was looking for! This is heaven on earth! And this feeling mostly comes to us naturally when we don't force this to happen this way or that way, when we just allow certain positive energy to lead our path of life.

We need to learn the art of differentiating situations as when to allow things to blossom beautifully like a rose and when to cut out some ugly thrones of the stem. It is all within us the path to eternal love, eternal happiness and freedom till eternity it's all just within us only, within our mind & soul. We can learn this only through connecting with our soul. It will provide us the desired notifications as when to look out for ways to control the situations and when to allow things to flow in the way they want to. For that we need to see things on a deeper level with multiple dimensions of perspective. What is leading to what? How they are moving and why they are moving this way only? What could have been better and why? Is this for the best? How I am going to manage this elegantly? And so many other questions that you need to create within yourself. Choose to look both at brighter and darker sides of things and choose walk only at the brighter path, having a look at the darker side will teach us the difference in appearance of the both paths so as to make it easier for us to walk on the bright path.

Create the art of self-analysis within you to magnify the rays of divine that we carry with us.

Choose to experience freedom at the soul level which will last till eternity. Change it from an experience of a vacation of a month or two or an outing for a day to an evergreen one, where you flow freely with the universal energies. Bring in this change slowly at your own pace of doing things as things are best experienced when we do it at our own speed.

Remember rushing back home from school, jumping on your sofa and watching your favourite TV show, just with an honestly happy state of mind, not worried about what's next to face or encounter with, just so lost in happiness of the present moment. We feel such relaxed happiness within us at that point because our mind has the idea that we are free from school for the day. Even if we know we have to follow the same schedule of schooling tomorrow but we are so lost in the idea of freedom of the day that we hardly care for any tomorrow. We all need to get that lost within our soul that rest everything should appear as blur as the probability chapter. Moving closer towards our soulful journey on earth will help us to maintain our daily life with a healthy state of mind, where we are decently happy with what we have, working with positivity to acquire what we don't have and growing beautifully with a flourishing mind and a happy heart.

Chapter 3

We humans mostly find ourselves drowning in sad emotions when left alone or when we decide to stay alone, our unhappy memories hang around us to make us feel low and terrific. That's when we keep on moving back and forth with the choice of being with ourselves or around too many people. But the day when we will be left alone yet honestly happy and involved in some productive work or creative work that will be the day to make us realise the worth of the self-growth and soul work that we have done on ourselves. From that day onwards we won't be searching for freedom or intense happiness in the outside world. We will be living each moment of our life with that freedom shining through our soul. We will be witnessing the magic of real freedom within us.

Whatever we search for in this life is the reflection of our inner person who wants to experience those certain kinds of things. Sometimes we are aware of it truly while at others we just get attracted to them by various means. Whatever may be the way of moving into something that is attracting us or even if we are going there willingly if that brings the honest and hardest smile on our face then it is worthy of anything and everything.

The sense of living balanced life is the phrase that best describes real freedom. The sense of balanced life here means when to take the lead in life and when to back off for the universe to take the lead is the real freedom. Once we get to realise these set of senses as per which we can blindly trust our instincts and follow the natural process of life as we see it through our eyes, we will be capable enough to witness genuine freedom in a unique frame. Here are some instances, when you are experiencing any unpleasant or not rightly serving your energy kind of circumstances, you will sense the presence of those instructions in your mind as what to do and how to do in order to manage things smoothly. As it enables us to excel in life the way we had dreamed of or more beautifully. Sometimes working hard to get things turn the way you want them to and then sometimes letting the universe to unwrap your gifts from the divine. Everything takes time having patience and the ability to see things as the universe wants us to see them through connecting more with our soul is what makes us so different than others.

Getting to understand that balance thoroughly and implementing it in the exact accuracy even in the presence of people is the skill that will take us into a journey of witnessing incredibly outstanding magic in the real world. This will also set our soul free from certain unpleasant blamings, repressed emotions or any other kind of tough feelings that we were meant to go through any way. Those negative energies are part of the journey we should allow them to come and go with love and grace.

Chapter 4

Many of us live life without expecting good things from life because things haven't turned out the way they intended it to be, repeatedly or since a very long time. Living life without expectations is the best way to live life but leaving expectations should not be done in a negative way. No expectations, yet celebrating the little signs or gifts of divine silently with utmost gratitude is what enables us to attract more positivity and abundance in life. Showing gratitude towards minute pleasures of life will set us free from all forms of worries and emotional baggage. Gratitude is the language through which we can directly converse with the universe. Sinking deep into the feelings and experiences of life to learn the art of shaping them as per our requirement to install real freedom that will last an entire lifetime on earth is what we should learn quickly so that we can start living life in a new and exciting way.

Things that come to us naturally are the ones that lasts longer than our expectations. Naturally means when our focus was not at that particular aspect of life but somehow it came to us as a guide or with any other form of positive energy. This is how gifts of universe come to us at the most unexpected moments yet expected moments. when we are aware things are going to get done in a way but we are not aware of the exact way that's how we bump into another gift of universe. Here is the situation of showing gratitude towards the universe that I was trying to explain.

We need to learn the difference between trying and forcing things to happen and the exact way for them to take place. Trying is a positive thing. We all should go on trying different ways that will take us somewhere better than where we are now and the want for growth and advancement is always appreciable. But at a certain degree it becomes forcing when we unknowingly cross that thin bar between the two. Wants and desires are good, having something set in mind is good too but they become better or best when kindled with flexibility. At certain points the correct awareness of the right degree of flexibility with our ideas, wants and desire also have the ability to set us free from wasting a lot of our energies into things at the wrong timing or in the wrong way. Here the true connection with our soul and our self will make us aware of when we are setting our first foot into forcing from trying. Our energies are the way we connect with the world and the way we present ourselves to the world. We should subtly learn the fine art of conserving our energies and using them in the exact impressive way that suits the personality we have created in our mind about who we are. We can best identify the perfect use of our energies by the connection we have acquired with our soul.

The universe enlightens our thoughts, words and ideas, most of us might have the idea that if we keep on saying, wishing or praying for somethings repeatedly it happens over time. On basis of this I will share two ideas.

One is if we decide to set ourselves free from bad thoughts and will start praying and wishing for good things only then with time that positivity will get aligned with our real-life incidents. Let's make it a daily habit of at least trying out if we are able to add some of the goodness and remove a bit of negativity as per our ease. And it's not possible for anyone to just delete and simultaneously add new things or ideas on daily basis even once in a month too. Because we are living with ideas that we have since so many years and it is not so easy to change them but, surely, we can modify then slowly and gradually through daily prayers. Daily prayers that we do in our households save us from so many unseen evil forces out there. Similarly daily wishes of growth will at least keep you away from evil from the very 1st day, this slight movement is success that we should identify and celebrate. The desire for betterment will set us free from old rusty ideas that don't serve for our free will of growth.

And the second idea is if universe is able to listen to our plans for life, our ideas on how to live life then we can also listen to its plan which it has stored for us. This is something that need specialised connection with the universe from the soul level as soul is the only thing that is most closely connected to the realms of universe. This needs higher degree of meditation like those of saints to get acknowledged with the true purpose of our birth on earth. Or by the gift of universe itself some of us are lucky enough to get aware of the true purpose and what they are here to do and how to do. There are many reasons how some individuals just feel that they have this to do and only this to do and the way even after living a normal everyday life. They are mostly the self-immersed kind of people; they focus on their life in such an intensely positive way that any distraction can hardly get their attention. Such individuals look at the world through a positive yet clear about the fact's kind of prism. Those people have walked down half or more on the path of finding themselves. They have managed to create a strong connection with this life of theirs at an ultimately deep level by experiencing everything from the root level whatever life has thrown at them. We need to learn the way these individuals carry themselves so as to dig deeper into our lives.

Chapter 5

We all long for a carefree and happy life, because the idea of it gives a sense of relaxation in our mind even in a sorrowful moment. That sense, that idea or tiny ways of creating them will only last for a few moments or for a certain number of days. But if we want to fix it permanently, we have to acquire wisdom along with knowledge. Wisdom is something that we learn as we live through situations or circumstances that either test our ability to cope or provides us support to cope. Wisdom will make us understand things why they are as they are, what is saving us from what and how and lot more things that we haven't even thought of. Wisdom will make us realise that freedom is not something that sets us free from responsibilities rather it is the way of accepting our duty on earth with a happy heart and an enthusiastic mind. Wisdom is like our identity card that gives us identity of what we are capable of and the degree of our capability too can be well explained by it.

Wisdom is the way we can easily connect with our 'self', our soul, our heart, our mind and they all together collectively can be well interlinked through wisdom. This simple word holds the power and strength to set us free from every kind of mental breakdown, failures, disappointments, unworthy feelings, negative energies, setbacks and everything else that create hinderance in the path of a carefree and happy life. Wisdom is like air not visible but always present in everything how big or how small, no matter what, its presence is visible to people who seek to look out for it not to those who keep their eyes of mind closed. It is present in everything that we see everything that we witness, let's make the choice to look out for it.

How to set ourselves free in each and every situation by using wisdom? Here is a way to understand it if each situation is like a bundle of sealed papers, then wisdom is that seal, we have to open it by acquiring wisdom and go through each paper from both the sides to enhance our wisdom level. Those papers are multiple interdisciplinary ways of understanding circumstances by using higher perspectives. At this point of life if we want to add wisdom which we haven't gained yet then we need to examine every past and present scenario from as many dimensions of as many people involved in it, things like what was their intentions and what was their actions; how it impacted us and why; why we allowed them to treat us as they did; what our inner voice is saying about this analysis and what should be the new way or is it ok to proceed with the present one. While we will start adding this analysis in our daily routine with an objective to find out the traces of positivity that surrounds us it will lead us on the glorious path of finding ourselves. The search for our self is nothing more than identifying the roots of our happiness, identifying energies that satisfy the purpose of our life at the soul level. As we will gradually learn about what serves our energies better; what are the ways we want to get treated with and by whom; how to react to things as per the circumstances and with respect to our personalities. Wisdom is nothing more than enhancing the power of self-realisation of things which we used to turn our eyes blind on them, just learning the correct angle of opening our eyes to particular objects is what it means to acquire wisdom. It should be acquired, nourished and well protected from the world around us in many instances. It needs to get projected as per the requirement. Wisdom can be best acquired and finely projected when we are well aware of our own worth, not overly thought and not too lowly, a perfect realisation of self-worth is must to have it beautifully crafted in our mind and applied in life.

We need to create the definition of freedom for ourselves from the wisdom that we acquire by the process of our life and not by how it is imparted to us or visualised in the world around us. None of us do live life in same ways then how can the meaning of freedom be same for all. We all are living our lives with problems and blessings that suits our unique range of energies then our picturization of freedom should also be unique as per our views of life.

By removing our attention from life of others and just focusing on ours will set us free from so many unwanted desires, longings and the greed of that particular kind of happiness the other person is experiencing. Well fascination is good, desires are good too but they should not overplay their roles, again here wisdom will play its role to make you realise when to stop over fascinating or over desire of things when they are moving towards bad terms. Our should always aim to achieve things in the best positive path which doesn't even carry a pinch of negativity in it because negative energies always try to follow us wherever we move to, so to keep additional negativity away we need to opt for the positive path every time.

Chapter 6

Let's find out what real freedom is for us, there's no point of accepting freedom as the world points it out to be, if we haven't even thought of the definition of freedom by using our freedom then of course that is not the real freedom for us. Believe in your ideas more than what others teach you to carry. Allow yourself to accept your 'self'. Be true to your own ideas of living, goals with an urge to modify them for the greatest good. Find out your own potentials and grounds that resemble your strength use them to transform your life gradually but surely. Let's set ourselves free from expectations and disappointments and raise the hunger of reaching that extreme level of freedom in life by such good means that nothing can bring us down.

Enhance the beauty of that free soul within you. Let it glow with the colours of self-analysis, wisdom and rectification. Let the balance by the connection to your soul ease the path of life for you, give the universe the required time to move pieces for you. Till then focus on what you have on your list to work at and meanwhile applying the magic wand of gratitude towards every tiny blessing that are trying to make your days way better.

Let's make peace with the gentle flow of life as the rewards, blessings, abundance that we never saw coming will one day light up our lives in the way we never even dreamt of. Until then let's keep it real and true to the things or people in our lives that matters to us, most importantly let's be true to ourselves. Let's live it in the way we wish to live it. Not even a tiny burden of fakeness should be allowed to ruin even a bit of our part of happiness. Let's choose to build up and increase our talents to use them as wings to fly high. Let's make the word 'unstoppable' as our soul reason for existence.

Let's set our own meaning, definition and rules of real freedom. Let's make it something like the life boat that will mean to set us free from even the worst adverse situations too. Let's make it such a powerful tool which will act as our saviour in hard times and eventually not the reason of facing hard times. Let's beautify with love and responsibility of our well-wishers. Let's change its whole dimension and outlook such that it serves for our best interest. Let's consider it as a gateway that opens with true wisdom as we let go of our mind from being afraid and worried about worthless ideas.

Give it a start from very small things by gradually modifying the ways in which we see normal everyday things. See minute objects as token of love, affection and care from the divine. Start taking things I positive ways focusing more on what it is leading to not on what it is looking like at the particular moment. Just a bit of encouragement and believe on the self can bring such huge transformations in our lives that we can never think of. Let's take a pinch of self-belief and blend it with wisdom to explore what's within and what surrounds us in order to find out what is real freedom for each one of us.

Let's take time to realise when to leave our freedom in the hands of time and divine. Let's take off the burden of taking lead when it is not so necessary. Let's be wise enough to determine our time of taking rest in life and time of preparing hard for future events. Obstacles that come in the path of our ideas of freedom might seem to create a negative circle around us but actually they are protecting us from those unseen dangers and simultaneously creating that majestic path of auspicious happiness which is beyond our fascination.

Everything that we are searching in the outer world are only reflections of those ideas that we have experienced in our past lives and we have certain parts of them within us in this life too. Real freedom is actually when we acknowledge that we have to align together those parts of free and happy ideas within us and make a strong relation with them until we naturally come across the other parts as life unfolds itself. Enjoy life as it is moving no matter how slow or how fast. Let's be in the moment and get involved with things on the basis of how they inspire us for better. Let's change the dimension of freedom as something like breakout to something like living in the moment with wisdom. Let's change it from an experience of certain months or years to a lifetime experience of joy and honest happiness. Let's make it a long lasting and evergreen idea of living. Let's sit back and observe real freedom walking towards us, wishing to impart its gentle warmth into us. Let's change it from something that creates thrill in our soul to as something that magnifies the gentility of life.

Let yourself to be silently drawn towards it.

CHAPTER SIX

WHY DO WE FEAR TO ACCEPT OUR FAULTS?

Chapter 1

As humans we have some inbuilt faults in our behaviours, way of thinking and analysing and some bad decisions which come out just due to the heat of the moment. The faults in our features play many roles in the flow of our lives respectively. Some of them harm us in different ways by letting us drown in bad feelings, and due to our basic tendency to see certain things in certain ways for which we just can't avoid them many a time. While other of them affect the people in our surrounding in harmful ways through the words we speak, the pitch of our speech or actions that we perform in a manner because of our intrinsic tendency of doing them in such ways. Faults are always the one that we do subconsciously not those which are deliberately done to harm others. Faults are the one that just pop up without our knowledge or proper attention.

Most of the time we are not aware of their existence until we encounter a far better platform of living life. As we gradually move into better surroundings with better people, we gradually realise our faulty features and wish to change them, making them alike to that of others. Faulty features are like invisible gates, until we search for them, they won't appear in front of us. As in the case of looking out for rays of growth makes the gates of self-growth appear in front of us, one by one. Similarly in case of faults also we need to look inside our features thoroughly in order to gradually identify them and clear them out not as soon as possible and make them as better as possible. Because if we aim to refine them in a way that they won't be able to find us once again then our method should be impactful and time taking. We all are here on a mission for certain degree of development of our soul towards goodness and divine light in this lifetime. Here I mentioned our method should be time taking because we are living this life as another chance given to our soul for growth and faulty features need time to be eradicated with love and final goodbye.

We need to search for them not by comparing ourselves with other rather by observing the impact of our actions, speeches, facial expression and way of interaction on our mind and on our surrounding. What impact they are creating on our surrounding? What is better than this? What can serve our mind in a better way? What is the closest possible positive change available for this?

None of us is living a 100% perfect life from that deep level of soul. Each one of us are carrying a few faults within us. And almost everyone on this planet encounters certain negative energies once or more depending on our capability to face them. Those negative energies at the time of leaving, leave us with a gift of realisation about what went wrong, how and when our faults played their role. We face them according to our capabilities and thus we realise and change too according to our strength, so the more we are capable of facing negativity the more we are capable of moving towards divinity. That doesn't mean that we need to force ourselves rather we should allow our soul to make its way as it wants to proceed.

Faults are nothing to be ashamed of until they aren't harming others. It is just the way we were brought down to earth but that doesn't mean we have no control over them, we need to gain control over ourselves to manage them properly. And that needs delving deeper into ourselves. First, we need to prepare our mind to identify and accept our faults with a happy state. For that the basic fundamental need is to build up our mind to a good and mature enough state to carry out the task. The time that our mind takes to reach that state varies from person to person. There is nothing much that we can do it according to our mood or wants in this case, that state of willingness in our mind to accept our faults comes to us as per the set time of divine. But the state of free will always give some space to our choices and desires. If in that free state we will choose to look more into what is within our 'self' that is causing harm to our humanitarian feelings, then that might act as a catalyst to pull the time, set by the divine for us to, a bit closer or the level of soul enhancement in this lifetime may also move to a higher degree than that would have actually been.

The most common kind of fault that almost every one of us has experienced is how we let certain things affect our mind. It is a critical idea of fault as it creates so many ways of misinterpretations. If while sitting in a class we are listening to the teacher but at a certain point we have made our mind agree that 'I will listen to it but I will thoroughly examine that thing at home.' Then that fixed idea will not allow you to get completely involved in the class with 100% attention. You will pay attention but only to important points or just headings, you won't be able to get deeply involved with the perspective and ideas of that particular teacher. This is not a wise idea instead it is a fault; we need to allow those things meant for upgradation of our knowledge and wisdom to completely flow into our minds without any hinderance. We need to thoroughly examine things at that particular moment only, nothing should be kept for latter, other person's better ideas need to get crafted in our mind keeping the faults miles apart.

If we will start focusing on extracting the finest possible outcomes of every moment then somehow, gradually, we will start walking on the path of moving away from our faults. As we won't let ourselves be confined in our old rigid thoughts and way of working, we will look up at what a level up thing is and how to install it within us. Confinement is the reason why most of us are not aware of their faulty features. Confinement is good when we are surrounded by lower energy vibrations as it will act as a shield there then. But when we are put up to a good or better sphere of energy than ours, there we ought to remove that confinement and welcome levelling up of our features.

Here too the sense of realisation when to build up and when to release confinement also needs our special connection with what level of our energies are? Start it from analysing from different people around you, what are their occupations, what is their way of living and interacting with people of different standards of the society. If you are not in favour of analysing other people then go for examining situations and your feelings and your mind set with respect to them. After observing them, take into account what best serves your interest of living life as a gift of nature, though casual and usual but having that tiny spark of magical aura of divine. Accept what serves right to your mind and soul, keep it intact even at adversity. Construct small steps of analysing, realising and accepting. Move slower but definitely higher on them. Set an average pace of creating your way of interacting and surviving in the society as a decent human. As decency is best created when mind is devoted to the divine power.

Chapter 2

There are times when we feel highly ashamed of our faults when they appear in front of many people, we think the day went wrong and carry that baggage of ashamed feeling for certain days and then we continue to be so as we were. No, we need change, we are not here to just continue living with them or make ourselves feel comfortable to be with the faults. We are here for levelling up our features and anyhow we are going to do that the circumstances will compel us to do that, so it is better to do it when we witness the first red flag. Dig deep about what thoughts are leading the faults to come up to the surface. We need to transmute those thought processes that are causing the fault to take 3D shape, into nearest step of levelling up.

Here the idea is a bit complicated if will hold on to them for long they will stick to us more boldly, if we will ignore them, they will again come up at similar situations. Hence, while dealing with faults we should bring up some intellect and smartness to tackle them. What I want to convey is we can completely remove them out by applying a smart idea, that is, hold on to them on the days you feel most ashamed of, hold on to it for the entire day, examine the responsible thoughts, create a barrier in mind for not letting those thoughts to begin their evolution process in your mind. And the next day recheck it from time to time if they are moving in the same manner or you have successfully made the change. If you have made the change successfully then, congrats! and if you haven't, then continue the process until a significant level of change is experienced. And if it is not working even after repeated trials then don't cling on to it much as excessive trials ruins the entire experiment leaving it in damaged mode for a long time. Wait for next time when you will face the fault coming on to the surface by itself. This time ask yourself what you want to do apply the above method or something else.

Another good alternative is transforming the entire vision of our mind regarding that particular thing, for which the fault is appearing, into a uniquely beautiful and appealing one. Changing the entire concept is always the most trusted and effective way of making things better or right. No doubt that new sheet should be far more renowned one that the present, this should be something that is found more in people of good thoughts and divine rays.

One thing that we can mark on the days we feel ashamed due to faulty features is that our mind develops the desire to look deep into us and our heart wishes to spend some time alone. Despite the presence of good peeps who are willing to uplift our mind we still feel the desire to correct those strings of faulty thoughts. And that desire is of great importance which should be taken care of on that very day.

We are born into a world where we don't have much awareness about the way of living life, as we grow, we learn from the world around us and in the mean time we forget to connect with ourselves because nobody taught us to do that. They just taught us to do things in this way or that way. No one pointed that we ourself, our existence itself is a magic of the universe and slowly we have to get closer to ourselves. Only life teaches us that through good or bad circumstances. We learn who we are through our faults only, as that desire of rectification arising from those faults which leads us on that path of self-evolution.

We all know how snakes shed their old skin and acquire new one from time to time, we humans who live with the objective of self-growth also do the same with our personality, thought process and perceptions. Likewise, faults are meant to get shedded and upgraded at a regular interval. Our lives are not always confined to one kind of energy background so even if we are comfortable with some of our features when we move to a new background, we shouldn't feel reluctant in upgrading them, always opt for an uplifting change. Nature always has numerous signs and secret messages for us to interpret them in our ways. Have you observed how the waves of the sea runs towards us to kiss our feet with its salty water, actually it washes all the dirt from our feet to make it clean even while standing on sand, here the nature tries to do two things one is to remind us how pampering is its love and second to keep us clean in every aspect, even when dirt is just below our feet?

Observe nature when you feel low on energy or low on faulty days to find out ways of up lifting your mood while ensuring positive outlook on both nature and yourself. The beauty of the universe is even if it wants us to learn living by ourselves it still tries to hold our hands in hard times, feel that presence of unconditional love for you, have that blind faith on universe to love you even at your worst. Even when you are not able to accept your faults the universe still has the audacity to provide you the love of entire world. Believe in the caring nature of earth.

Chapter 3

'Consciousness of the self' is the term that can work as a compass to locate our faulty features in the ocean of life. Imagine that you are the only sailor sailing yourself in an ocean with high and uneven waves, in a motor boat. Question yourself how you are going to get through those merciless waves when you have only one chance to get through them if you are successful, you are alive, if you aren't, then you know the result. Only thing that can save you is the presence of mind and awareness of what you need. Now relate those merciless waves with your faulty features because some of our faulty features at some important times actually spoil what was ahead of us, mostly they are certain dreamy opportunities that we had long wished for.

Some of our faulty features have the capability to alter the path of our life to a lane lower than before. If we get to experience this obviously that fault will create a lifetime effect on our mind and taking it to go for a positive change or not, depends on our perspective. There are events in life of almost everyone that create a bad feeling but we can't deny the fact that those are the reason we improve to what we are. Yes, faulty features may take you down but again the sailor in you need to sail right to set you free from that by using the compass of consciousness of the self. Ok now let's have look what does that term convey-standing firm and rooting for goodness within the self of our, being consciously aware of the right path that our self wants to follow, being rightly connected to our sense of following the positivity within and around us, realising the range of energies that we radiate, analysing the impact that we create, truly aware of the path that we prefer and are walking on, analysing the ripple effects of our thoughts, connecting deep with the vibrations that we feel and realising the level of nourishment that we look for. These concepts all together form the base for this term. No doubt there are endless concepts that can come under this term but more over on an overall basis these are a major part of what the term indicates.

When we start focusing more on the consciousness of the self, we get aligned with everything within us that constitute to give the idea of 'the self'. As we will move deeper in every aspect to find out what we are made up of eventually we will find out our strengths and faults too. There are no other short cuts to find out our faults are other than using this path of having an entire overlook on the self which can only make us aware of every kind of faults that we carry within us. But again, to recognise them as faults we should have that basic insight on what a better self should look like as per the time of the society we live in and our place in that. Hence in order to make this consciousness effective on us our mind should have a proper amalgamation of outer idea of living and the inner self.

We all are sailing in the same sea with just different boats having different features and speeds, we have to focus on managing our own's and not to get distracted by other's speed or high-tech features. What we have is representing what we are capable of handling at that particular stage of life. And if we want to have a better one then first, we need to master at what has been provided to us. The only intention of almighty is to make us perfectly excellent in what we are doing, as we will focus on doing better and better things will also turn better and better. This focus on us will keep us away from any kind of distractions and let-down feelings. And hence we excel in our job. All I want to say is using the term -consciousness of the self, we will make our mind well focused on our mission of life and doing it in our way that is the immediate brilliant path lying next to us.

One of the greatest faults that most of us carry is that we are not even aware of the need to connect with the 'self'. We just flow with the ideas of the people that surrounds us or invites us in an appealing manner. We are more attracted towards having fun with people rather than accepting and respecting the fact that we need to hold our hands first through the analysis of what is within our mind and soul.

Let's stop getting swayed by the opinions of others. Let's be alert of what our 'self' has to say to us. Let's build up the antibodies of detecting the faults within us by finding out what features best suits our personality.

Consciousness of the self can also be understood as the way to look at ourselves from the eyes of a viewer or 2nd person. That is opening the third eye and visualising how we look when we project our faulty features and also the good features. Just acquiring the overall visual picture and being clearly able to point out everything in details about what we are and how we are representing ourselves. Considering ourself to be on the spotlight from time to time and then minutely examining ourselves will make us knowledgeable of the self.

Moreover, the term consciousness of the self relates to the detailed idea of a person on his/her inner self, outer representation of the self and the medium or the ways he/she connects his/her inner self with outer world that is perception. It is too difficult to gain desired control on all of these at once that is why we keep on dwelling back and forth from here to there from beginning to beginning.

We keep on losing and gaining hope from time to time for things to change but if we have the concept of moving towards positive light constant then this dwelling will also prove to be worthy at divine timing.

Chapter 4

There are so many confusions and questions that comes to our mind while interacting with people but along with the passing years on earth we learn a lot of things about interacting with people. Many of the times our features or qualities get affected by people with whom we interact excitedly or consider that we feel good around them and sometimes our inner self gets adversely affected by the qualities of others. All these exchanges of qualities and features takes place when we haven't prepared a proper concrete wall to protect our good qualities and haven't done enough work on our faulty features. Even at times our faulty features start to grow in presence of certain individuals when we are unaware of that influence. Then here a question arises about- how to protect our 'self' from the influence of other people when we are still working on it?

Whenever we are interacting with someone new or from now on everyone around us-observe their arrangements of words, preferences of words, placement of 'I', 'you' and 'us', degree of benevolence towards you and others, their body language while speaking and interacting, their tone in different sentences, their pitch, the moment of their eye balls, their way of protecting their views, their popular method for standing up for themselves, their frequently used formula for the field you are present in, their facial expressions at different times and a lot more things to look at before letting their personality affect what's within you. We should have that degree of alertness of our mind to mark all of them at once and decide how to deal with them in a cool way but at the same time not letting them affect us in any bad way.

Our faulty features when they come in contact with similar vibe, they grow to get stronger and magnify. And as the process is slow, many a times we find it familiar and won't be able to spot out any visible difference in our features. We only realise them after a huge rock crashes our mind and leave our senses opened. But before that happens let's learn to give second thoughts before interacting and speaking to people. Let's learn to figure out how to treat individuals as per our relative energy vibrations with them. We can't let our faults to grow at any cost even for a single moment and even the thought of being surrounded by such individuals who let them grow is so painful for our soul's mission on earth, we can't afford to lose our shine. We are here to sparkle like a star removing all ugly spots that aren't letting even a single ray of ours to spread light. We are here to get rid of everything that can't serve for our soul's progress, not even a single compromise is to be tolerated. There are people who think tolerance will give them peace and suffer many violent crimes happening on them, I would like to say them, you are also the child of universe try taking a step ahead to help yourself get free from suffering, just take that one little step and the universe will come up with world class magic to turn your life into a fairy tale. Not only violence in terms of behaviours, attitudes and many other things many good people have a habit of being quite when someone proudly shows his/her faulty features. No, by remaining quite we are doing wrong to both our 'self' and that person. Our 'self' is suffering because it doesn't want to be in that state of energy and about the other person, we can't change anyone, it can be done with their will power only, but we should at least make that person completely aware of that faulty nature and how it is ruining him/her. And if that person is still unable to go for a change, then the last option that we have is to distance ourselves from such individuals as protecting the progress of our features is also a moral duty that we have to do for our 'self'.

I believe protecting our level of thinking and living is more important than growth because preserving the work already done on the self will let us work on it more tomorrow. But if we are unable to protect what work we have already done then we will continue to work and work at the same point till eternity. Don't look down at people who you feel as radiating relatively lower kind of energy than yours rather prefer to look up at people with relatively higher energy level. As we are living with the hunger of growth that we have created within us we shouldn't even think about people of lower energy level as we really have a long list of to do work on the 'self'. Even a bit of liberality towards collaborating development of our faulty features with negative energies will prove to be hazardous on us. To check the advancement of our faulty features is the one of the primary steps of self-care.

Life moves on with continuous addition of responsibilities and tasks to do one after another. With addition of responsibilities life gradually becomes complex and the level only increases so as our progress. But as things get levelled up in terms of toughness, we learn better how to protect our peace, may be that's the beauty of that divine light within us, the soul. Protecting our identity at required times should be enlisted as vital for our survival like any other daily needs such as food and water. In my earlier chapters I was discussing more about the importance of growth, now let's learn how to protect them. Apply your unique ways of creating better feelings by using better features within you more frequently so that it becomes a part of your daily routine and move up to that stage when you will find it uncomfortable while not applying those good qualities daily. Manifestations of self-growth can be considered as an easier task over the task of maintaining them and keeping them unaffected by lower vibrational energies till the end. While mentioning about this task addition of progress seems to be a far-fetched goal. Here let the mind's desire to be unstoppable take over the process of progress and preservation of it. Consciousness of the self, combined with will power along with good mental health has the ability to bring in more rays of divine to merge with our soul. Peaceful yet progressive state of mind has enormous amount of power to enable us understand the vast pretext of our way of interacting with ourselves and others.

Chapter 5

In the path of finding and clearing our faults we will face faults of different levels and varieties. At some points, many of our faults are not so easy to deal with. Those are so intensely aligned with our self that they act as great obstacles for us when we try to move higher in life. At such points there comes a state between the states of finding out our faulty features and working on them called 'acceptance'. Accepting the faults for good with an intention to work on them slowly but surely concept and not being rude on our self. Acceptance is not as easy as it sounds here, our inner self should be capable enough to look at our self from such a low point and still love it for that time being with a hope of positive change. This requires a definite amount of faith on the self, not confidence just faith and comparatively more amount of love for it. The harder the trouble the smoother and gentle the effort should be. I have heard, there is a proverb-silent and steady water can cut even huge stones into pieces, gently accepting them with love and changing them with care over time will be like experiencing a magical journey within our 'self'.

Acceptance should be brought along with appreciation of the 'self'. As we appreciate with good intentions we start to bloom with wisdom. If the pleasure of acceptance moves parallel with the desire of growth, then the lane of life begins to move from tiring to playful. The will of being a better person tomorrow should be greater than finding a reason to survive. Acceptance is like power of the eyes of our mind that will help us to clear the blurry picture of our 'self' in mind. As the level of acceptance increases, the image of the 'self' starts to move from 144p to 240p then 360p and so on.

Have you seen minute dust particles on the surface of the mirror if left untouched for a few days, acceptance is like removing those dust particles and strongly attempting to see the marks of our face aiming to work on them with love and care?

The stage of acceptance is a bit tensing as we have to stay alert on how much we are letting it to have some space until we are prepared enough to change them for forever. Before starting to accept our faults, we ought to set a standard degree for acceptance not more nor less just up to the mark. This time we have to stand rigid on the border separating the two levels of acceptance, those are, one where we get so indulged that we forget that it needs to be changed and second when we are aware of the fact that it has to undergo a vast change in future.

It would be much better if we will first take our required time to create a drawing sheet in mind, of what acceptance looks like, as here acceptance has to serve for something which will have a huge impact on us, only after setting the goal of self-improvement. Take time to create it with affection and decorate it with the ornament of wisdom. To keep it unaffected from outer influences we have to completely wipe out the idea of getting judged while taking the first step of this process.

Peace is the word that is coming to my mind to explain it better, make peace with yourself and your surrounding within your mind. As it will let you focus on what's on your mind with much efficiency than before. If you are experiencing things that tigger your mind while you are trying to work out on this then go for instant meditation no matter what the time it is just do it and bring that peace to relax the inner you. Acceptance combined with peace will elevate our level of spirituality into folds higher.

What is that fear that we face while accepting them?

Sometimes while facing the clear image of our faults through acceptance, we get afraid of negative consequences of our own faults. It is that same thing that we have been living with since so many years, and that idea of existing with it sometimes shakes our heart out. It brings the question of bravery to the surface. But the word of the wise here would be to kneel down in front of it and beg pardon to your 'self' for suffering alone without your awareness. By staying low with acceptance at this point, with desire of positivity in mind we are letting the negative energy of the fault to grow weaker on us. Now while being in such a perilous state, we have to proceed smoothly, kneeling down to come up with a greater force and wiser us. One step back for two steps ahead.

But at the time of remaining low just stay low don't think about how you are going to make it better, just be in the moment to bear the pain with love and acceptance. This bearing mind set has the ability to forge small parts of all divine rays within you in a matter of days. The days of the present might be a bit tough to see yourself struggling as we still love our 'self' even when the faults are a part of it, we admire it and that's absolutely normal. We have unlimited rights to love our self and that's an integral part of our live.

Believe in the fact that no matter how downtrodden path we have walked on if we have done it with utmost sincerity and good intentions then positivity will always wait for us to give an equally warm welcome to all of us. Believe in the equal love of divine power. Make your mind understand that whatever may be the case you are safe the divinity is working for the best to give you the best. And so do you have to make the best decisions for your 'self'. Feel the power that is working in the background for us. Connect more to that background power to let the guides guide you towards enlightenment. Relate further in order to keep your steps more firmly than ever.

The next step is to let the gentle changes of life make us reach the shore. As by now we have accepted the faults and are working to change for better , life will take us on a gentle and smooth journey of gaining divine rays through dedication and good decisions. Just a small step of, accepting for good, can change the entire direction of flow of our life.

Now let me make the path of acceptance a bit easier for you by letting me talk to your heart directly, keep your mind shut for a few minutes now.

" Hi heart,

Hey, you! the tiny little creature! thank you for keeping your owner alive. I don't know you but I know how dedicated you are. I know you might have been through things that were tough for you but you have made your way until now. And you are capable of making your way through anything that is coming in your path. You are unstoppable and so your owner is. You have successfully kept your owner going even when you were at pain. You kept on working even when you were tired of this world. You haven't taken rest even for a sec since so long, hats off to your love for your owner. But your owner too, haven't taken rest that he/she actually needs. There will be a day when your owner will start taking care of your more than you are expecting. He/she will make her way to you and after that he/ she is going to love you like heaven for forever. And then you both will be at rest. Just hang in there for a few more rising and setting sun. One day he/ she will realise that all you wished for was love for the 'self'. Keep loving him/her until then as you are the only creature who is going to provide unconditional love until you stop working , one day."

Can we now accept and change for this tiny one?

We have to face the necessity of converting our faulty features into something so great that can bring a dreamy essence of pride within us. Do it with an intention to live a life of purity in heart, mind and soul. The thought of living with such purity is so calming and warm to feel. Changing only for that sake of the self and no other intention, just with a calm mind. Only to bring in the colours of peaceful life, so restful, so nourishing. Living only for the sake of living. Embracing only for the sake of embracing. Blooming only for the desire of blooming.

Sprinkle the essence of peaceful acceptance on the fear of facing faulty features.

CHAPTER SEVEN

WHY AREN'T WE ABLE TO EXPRESS OURSELVES?

Chapter 1

The simple idea of expressing ourselves involves mixture of all energies present within and outside us. Instant formation of our words at sudden moments defines our nature and feature. Many of us haven't focused on this aspect of human life. While some of us face problems in this side of life and for which they connect less or aren't capable of expressing brilliantly. There are so many reasons why many of us face problems in this.

One of the most common and widely popular reason is overthinking/over analysing, creating painful imaginary scenarios in mind. This happens when we are giving too much to the outer world than to ourselves because our 'self' always intents to bring peace within us and never creates the ripple effects of unwanted feelings. Rather it helps us to manage those unsteady waves of feelings. Whether the journey to the self or with the self both are calming and peaceful from the core. When we create imaginary scenarios by putting ourselves into circumstances that hardly has any relation with reality , we are experiencing a point in the dwelling process of our mind like that of the pendulum. Now think of a number line having both positive numbers and negative numbers. Sometimes our energies move from the positive side to negative and vise versa, and so does our mind and emotions. Some of us experience overthinking to such a great level that it makes them look at the world through the fog of it, they need to focus on 'the self' more that will help them clear it out, by meditating daily to build a strong base for mind.

Let me make it easier to understand there are mainly 2 types of overthinking that is, positive and negative. The positive overthinking involves ideas where we see ourself happy or flourishing in life in some way while following the wildest dreams of our soul. And the negative one as you are expecting it to be, the one that creates pain in our mind through fake images. When they come to us, we have to treat them with flexibility of mind as we certainly can't avoid energies coming to us. While encountering the negative overthinking we need to let it pass through as easy and smoothly as possible. And while going through the positive one we should get involved with it with a desire to make it come true.

Another reason is energy barrier. How each reader is going to connect with my work varies as per the relative energy level of mine and the reader. People who think alike or even partly alike with that of mine will connect with this text in the best and easiest way. But as the degree in difference of thinking will go on increasing the connection will go on decreasing.

We live our lives in that assigned peripherical energy level where fusion and fission of all our thoughts takes place. Only a few individuals manage to upgrade their level through consistent self-improvement methods and good vision of living with ethics and independently improved ideas.

Hence at times we face energy barriers where even if we have the right thought in mind, we won't be able to express rightly in front of specific individuals. As there might be a huge difference between their level of energy and ours. The greater the difference here the more scattered the interaction is. This sometimes occurs in vital arenas of life where we think it is really important for us to connect rightly but our energies don't co-operate. At times like this we have to form an analysis if we have to upgrade our level or it is just the way it is.

These barriers are of great importance as sometimes they protect us from something, sometimes they make us aware of alternate methods, at times they make us grow in a better way, sometimes we learn how to cope up with things, moreover they teach the entire management of life.

We have to make a clear analysis of all those energies that have been surrounding us since the beginning , what are the energies we get attracted to, what kinds of energies are present within us, what acts in favour of us and what not. Most of us gain these ideas as we live through, but at some points we forget to connect with this deep understanding of our life and then things start falling apart, being scattered. We have to maintain that connection with our transitional energies to move gently in life. We have to keep in mind the silhouette of our energies. Many of us are too lazy to waste our energy on things that won't work out for us, so let's make proper use of the power of analysis to bring in abundance and prosperity to our lives in the ways our energy best serves the purpose.

We can make some required changes on the overthinking front but in case of energy barriers we can only go for level up choice whenever it is available to us and in the other case, we will have to respect the difference and move on with life. Sometimes it is hard to respect the difference and move on because some of us might be emotionally attached to a person, that seems as a challenge to them. But at times like this universe is giving you a chance to learn balancing emotion with energy difference. You don't need to get strategic to balance them do it with grace because your only intention is to protect yourself from levelling down in the path of reaching 'you'.

We have to expand our consciousness based on our energy level of vibrations that we create from time to time, by being with the 'self'. Knowing the 'self' is a lifelong process and so is its growth. But before growth we have make a detailed research on our 'self'. How it functions also can interpreted as how we function with what objective in mind whether it is done consciously or that is just our nature. How we move from one energy level to another within our peripheral energy, through what means. How our energies get reciprocated by others or at different situations?

Chapter 2

'Me' what is the definition of this word? What is coming to your mind by listening to this word after going through some pages of this book? what are the best ideas through which you can define this word for yourself? 'Me' comprises of the baby you, the child you, the teen you, the adult you, the middle aged you and the old you all at once. How you have grown to; to become what; how beautifully you have managed until now; and how you are going to continue it in future? Everything since the past, the present, the future is just an overall idea of 'me'.

When you were a child how you used to react to things and how your reactions have changed so much along with the building up of a personality for yourself. How far you have travelled on the path of making a suitable personality within you. Rate it as per its good and bad qualities, are you happy with this or you want to put up some more qualities that will be superior than what's now.

Me is also about our performances that we have given or are giving on the stage of life. It is about how the range of delightful feelings that we feel as we re-watch our performances in life. The way we present ourselves as age modifies us. How we put our steps in uniquely different fields of life. In what direction we are moving with each step of ours. We can't take even a single step lightly as life can turn into anything in a matter of few seconds. The impact of each step has equal value in the measuring machine of the divine. Sometimes we need to take into account about the importance and vitality of the way we are putting our feet into things.

Now what about 'I'? I too can be considered similar to that of me but more precisely it gives the sense of 'who we are at present'. It can be defined as what 'me' is turning into in the present. For example, we use sentences such as- I am like this; I will choose this; I am going there, etc. 'I' mainly signifies the present 'me' according to our preferences and decisions at present.

By connecting intensely with 'me' we will get comfortable with who we are in virtue of which we can smoothly express our ideas as they are freshly created. As we will proceed to walk towards 'me' we will learn to provide ground to our thoughts, that is, we will be stable enough to not to get affected by anything.

When we will make a crystal-clear idea of 'me' and connect it with 'I' we will make ourselves turn into a person with too fine ideas of what the 'self' wants.

When we can add these ideas in mind after we have made our mind to undergo a process of cleansing from whatever influences or thoughts that aren't capable of making our dreams come true. Well, it sounds too easy than what actually needs to get done. As we all know how hard it is to control the flow of mind but that simple 'will' will make its way with time.

The amalgamation of our 'self' in terms of past, present and future with special focus on the present will increase our efficiency of self-expression. So, with the addition of new dimension to the words like 'me' and 'I' we can make the best arrangement of words that will serve the purpose of our speech with highest positivity.

Chapter 3

Our past traumas play as major obstacles on the path of finely expressing ourselves. They ignite those sensitive strings within us while under partly or exactly similar circumstances. Why they act as major barriers while expressing our views at certain times? Because some of us haven't healed completely from it. Why we haven't healed yet after yet after such a long gap? It is because until now we were not giving that segment of life enough time to get healed.

Physical wounds can be cleared out with the help of medical sciences but while talking about mental health, this healing of mind needs enough space and time. And only we can help ourselves, and that will be the most effective and healthy way of healing. It is as such because the all-time available person for you is only 'you'.

See we all know we attract circumstances as the way they come to us, sometimes it is because we are thinking too much about them and sometimes because we are seeing it as it is in our mind. As we see circumstances through the prism of our perspective, those strings try to pop-up through the help of our perspective and if our mind haven't healed completely then it will fall into this trap.

To reduce the burning influences of those traumas we have to make peace with them in such a smooth manner that they won't cause us anymore pain rather they will remind us how capable we are. By spending time with them we can reduce their impact on us in 2 ways. One is by letting them cause trauma as much they want to so that gradually their power on us will go on decreasing to nil. Second is fighting with them by collecting all that positivity and good spirit within us to make them too weak to create trauma. In either of the ways the result is the same. But it completely depends on our mental capability to decide which path to opt for. We can't differentiate here that weak people will opt for suffering instead of fighting boldly, because we never know what one has gone through. And even if it appears minute to others that might be a huge obstacle for that person. Whatever reason is making or portraying the other person to be weak, which I completely don't agree with, needs to get respected with true heart as whatever might be the case, he/she is not at a good phase. And even if he/she is at a good phase we still need to respect them along with their traumatic phase with the same spirit.

When someone opts for letting the trauma pass through them without creating any obstacles on the path of it, he/she will have to build a strong base to lean on as the bearing will require tremendous strength to stand firm on. And what is that base? Any guesses? Of course, that magnanimous form of self-love. Where you generously forgive everything and everyone who caused that trauma to you for your own sake and then simultaneously learning to bloom with every passing force of that trauma. Forgiving not to let them have their way to us again rather forgiving to completely remove them from our memory system. For creation of a new zone of memory filled with our achievements and trump cards. While being through that stage we have to provide our own warmth to our 'self' as to make it feel safe. We have to tightly embrace ourselves up keeping in mind that no amount of traumatic force will be able to break that bond of embracement. Strongly but gently pulling yourself up to that power of self-love where no negative vibrational frequencies can act straight on you. Creating a concrete room for your 'self' before letting it pass through you will protect you from those destructive vibrational frequencies of traumas. That concrete form of self-love will reduce the harmful effects of trauma up to a very negligible level, but to make it that easy to pass us our efforts on the formation of that concrete wall should be true to the core and smooth to put it on with grace.

Have you seen a ballet performance? How they do it so flawlessly after letting their feet bleed like river? It is their love and devotion for that art form that the blood seems so meaningless in front of it. Similarly, we have to lay the bricks of such a devotional form of self-love that the traumatic force will seem too weak in front of that power of love within us. Defeat that energy as elegantly as you are. You have opted for slowly winning over that energy so do it with smoothness and style. Observe the gentle moves of a ballet dancer and do it in that exact manner.

In the second way of fighting with it by bringing together all positive energy within us to minimize its impact involves standing in a boldly flexible way in front of it. Boldly so as that force up to a certain level won't be able to break us and flexible so that the force beyond our bold capability won't be able to wreck us up as we will use our win card of flexible movement of the mind. Boldness here refers to that strong determination to come out of it with overwhelming victory; and the flexibility here refers to applying our intelligence to apply it at excellent timings. Being wise while fighting with it will make us witness so much less of frightening situations that our future won't be much affected by its destructive forces. Our only aim is to face it off and clear it out from the path of our life with minimal damages.

Both the ways are equally effective in terms of successfully making our way out of those past traumas, the only difference is 1st one is slow and steady, and the second one is fast and furious with a positive spirit. After setting ourselves free from it we can easily communicate our views and opinions every time with zero resistance.

And one more important thing to remember while dealing with past traumas is to give your body and mind a proper eight-hour sleep as that will increase your efficiency up to twice at least. Take proper care of your physical and mental health as they are your only weapons and only survival kits.

Chapter 4

Before putting our thoughts into words, we have to make a choice what energy do we wish to release through them, is it negative or positive?

We all have read about the structure of atoms in our high school days. How electrons keep moving freely outside the nucleus in their respective energy levels and protons remain stably filled inside the nucleus. So do in our mind negative energies keep fluttering on the surface of it from time to time and positive ideas remain buried deep down under them, which can only be brought into words through paying close attention to them. The feature of negative energies is that they will try to create their vibrational frequencies as they aim to take over the control our mind. We have to maintain a healthy distance from those fluctuation. But it is only us with our 'self' has to protect our mind from getting drawn towards them. It doesn't take place at a regular basis but whenever it does, we have to be cautious about such changes in our state of mind by remaining close to the 'self'. We have to keep our mind and the 'self' compact to get a smooth control of expressing positivity. We have heard of the phrase- think before you speak; but I would like to redefine it as- connect before you speak, connect with the 'self' and positivity within you.

Moving on to-how can we remain close to the self and inner positivity in a permanently constant way?

Meditation is that magic in reality that will make our negative ideas[dirt particles] undergo the process of sedimentation and let the purity come up to the surface. The more the time given to the process of sedimentation the more purified it becomes. So, we have to do the exact same thing with our mind. As our common goal in life is to climb higher and higher so we have to purify and maintain the purity of both the 'self' and our surrounding constantly.

Our inbuilt energies will intend to drag us to speak words of that particular energy level. And it is really hard to overcome that dragging force within us when we are not satisfied with it or we wish to upgrade it. So, in order to pull the 'self' out of the impact of that force we have to work on that image of us in our mind that we want to truly exhibit for our own sake. We have to try forming our sentence based on that image while we are alone or not surrounded by many. With the practice of arrangement of words as per our desire to reshape the flow of positivity in our speech we can give a shinning outlook to our expression of ideas.

Always look out for people or opportunities those are going to inspire us to bring in the most drastically positive changes of our features as that will shape our 'self' with an incredible beauty.

Chapter 4

Sometimes we feel disconnected with our 'self' while putting our expressing ourselves. Those are the moments we are not true to our true 'self' in terms of our emotions and thoughts. It happens due to many reasons, mostly when we find the situation uncomfortable or when we are not around right individual who connect rightly with our thoughts.

At times like this if you are feeling like it is important to express rightly then go for it with positive spirit. Keep aside all negative thoughts about the results of expressing rightly because what we have to face, we will face one time or another, then it is completely on you to decide when you are ready to face it. And when you are feeling like it is not that important to express yourself rightly in front of those particular individuals or situation then just leave it as it is by remaining quiet.

But when the question arrives on protecting and finely representing our true 'self' through accurate expression of our feelings, emotions and thoughts, there should be any doubt about whether or not to speak up. Especially when our 'self' is taken as a target by someone whose energies ignite some negative energies within you. Here I am not asking you to put up a fight or something but rather asking you to protect your 'self' because only you can do it and only you have to do it.

Lack of proper expression of ideas also involves lack of confidence that is actually very common among the masses. For this we have to put high efforts on those grounds until we feel confident enough to project our comfortable 'self' through them. At this case work on the 'self' is the only way to level up the confidence.

Having a cheerful mind with enormous positivity will act as a rising elevator with all those work of self-rectification, self-growth, self-expression, clearing out negativity and walking down the lane to reach out to that divine light. Bye as humans we can't always be happy and cheerful, so, let's be hopeful.

Let's work on our every dull factor and while starting off we all will feel a low energy vibration but keep in mind every single human whoever is trying on something new is also experiencing the same low vibrational energy as that of yours. You are not weak, you are not dull, you are precious and you are worthy of every happiness that you desire. Don't just go on living with those dull features you have to bring a change and for that you have to wish for a change first. How can we wish for a better change if we are not aware of what is better than this? then start off your search mission of finding new and exciting ways of modifying your 'self'.

While we will opt for modifying the 'self' with amazingly pretty features our consciousness about the entire horizon of human life on earth will expand to its top levels. It would be a brand-new way of looking at the world and expressing in an outstandingly impressive manner.

Simply expanding of our knowledge about everything will add on to contribute on our ability to express in uniquely smart way.

Expand to express.

CHAPTER EIGHT

THE REST

Consciousness of the soul.

'Consciousness of the soul', some of you might have thought of how the book on the path to find yourself can end without mentioning this term. I had kept it for the end to make this a completely independent part to have a greater impact on the reader. This section is for 'rest' whatever questions you might be having in mind while starting to walk on the path to your 'self'.

Whatever words phrases terms that we come across as we were designed for or destined to. What energy presently you are in you are gaining something and losing something simultaneously. Mark what is that making you what you are or what you are becoming through what means. How your soul is feeling there? There is always something behind something going with us.

Now moving to the clarification of the term 'consciousness of the soul', it can be best explained as the way we are alert of the desires, aims, objectives and way of working of our soul. What is the first thought that comes to our mind or our soul feels when we witness something for the very first time. Like the fresh feelings that we feel as we start reading something or watching something. Those fresh feelings and thoughts are mainly directed by our soul, those initial ideas represent what we have within us. The term consciousness of the soul deals with connecting with that divine light like never before and too rare to be done by the common mass. We hardly get time from our busy lifestyle to connect with the soul but I believe it can be done along with our busy schedule by being true to ourselves at every moment of work, home, with family or friends, whatever it is whoever it is just go with the 1st thought provided by our soul. Listen to its gentle words as it is that unseen light which can see what our eyes can't. The power of our soul begins at the point where the power of our sense organs and normal human capability ends. It is the only part of human body that is a direct part of divine consciousness.

Moving on to how can we install this consciousness, first of all it is not something to get installed, it has to be brought up from within to the surface of mind. It has to be used as a field or ground where our mind will operate. Meditation or the fact of spending time with the 'self' remains constant here. While doing this we have to observe minutely-how our thoughts are moving? where are the starting points and end points? How they are unfolding in our mind? Which path they are opting for and in what time interval? How many of them are carrying positive power with them and how many are carrying negativity? Which one is making us happier and which one sad? How we are reacting to them? And what are the reasons we are reacting so to them? What relations our thoughts are having with societal and basic humanitarian values? Are they right enough to think about or not? Are they dangerous for us or the society? If yes, then why such things are coming? What they want to resonate? What impact they want to create on us or the society? What is the degree of divinity in them?

Put emphasis on how are your ideas associated with normal every day words like happiness, ceremony, playing games, approaching someone, starting a conversation, friendship, family, love, care etc, how good or how bad your ideas are, what kinds of feelings are they creating within you.

What is our thinking on how a particular thing should be done, and how it is actually done, what is our degree of correctness in it, what is the prefect idea of that and how far or how ahead we are from that perfectness, what are the most beautiful and most ugly pictures in our mind associated with that particular thing, how can we make our way to the best one?

Now for example, I am writing this book simply because I want to do it, personally I am not a voracious reader, there are many reasons why I am not, but here I want to put focus on this one – I don't like to put in my mind what others have to say , I love to listen what my inner voice or my soul wants to say to me. There are many friends of mine those who love to read books and there was a time when I wanted to inbuilt that habit but I failed, and thanks to that failure I am now writing this completely oriented on my original ideas. This was only my personal idea on book reading now you have to think what you want? what you soul wants? I will say a big 'no' if your mind is now opting for my idea of not reading books, there are many renowned writers who are voracious readers they manage to bring their original ideas after reading huge piles of books , I am just saying I am not one of them. You have to find out your tribe or your category of ideas and their position in the society.

What are our ways of interpreting words, signs and phrases in our mind? How the world sees them and how we see them? How unique or how common do we think? For example, look at this number for a 5 seconds- 1010, what you saw it as 10 and 10 or 1,0,1,0 or just 1010. In whatever way you saw it was your own way of seeing things. The relative degree of uniqueness and common features within you makes you see things as you see them.

We all talk about soul stating this and that but we are not clear about exactly where it is present in the human body. The fact is nobody knows, what I believe, 'we' from 'head to toe', the entire 'me', taking all the constituents of 'me' into account is the 'soul'. So, the term 'consciousness of the soul' is the 'consciousness of me' upon the base of 'divine light'. What power is providing power to the power house of each cell [mitochondria], what power is providing power to your body organs, some of you might be thinking it is food that we eat provide nutrients to our cell but what makes the cell accept those nutrients and work accordingly? It is that 'consciousness' in each cell that is keeping us alive. It is present in each cell of ours. It is that impulses and senses that we feel through each cell. We all are living, walking and talking rays of the divine. Do you still question how precious you are?

Not only in cells in all energies present within us and around us, that background force, that frontal one and from other four sides- right, left, up and down. That abiding force that lives with us from the moment we enter earth till the end. Those instincts, those thoughts, that will to do something, that perseverance and every tiniest thing present within us; every outer energy guiding us all together constitute to give the sense of-what our soul is like?

Consciousness of the soul is more about connecting to the soul every now and then. It is about focusing on the paradigms of our energies and the 'self' simultaneously. We have to do this by choosing to stay alert and our mind tilted towards the 'self'. We have to fix in mind that soul is the only divine power within us and by believing in its ideas we are truly and honestly moving on the path of dignity, rightness and prosperity.

Moving on to rest of the whys those keep peeking up in our mind while going through the process of life, has to do a lot with the connection that we will enhance with the soul day by day. We have to find our own answers through opting more to what the divine light within us has to say, rather than being one of the sheep in the herd. We have to make the habit of choosing the self an act that we can do even subconsciously.

We have to keep ourselves away from getting panicked while facing other difficult whys of life and if you are getting panicked then you have to raise up the degree of calmness and stability more and more. The connection with the soul will no doubt provide us enough wise abilities to go through anything and bloom like anything but even if something is troubling you, don't think that you have nothing more left to do, the path to the 'self' or the 'soul' is a never ending one. But if you are feeling like you have reached to it then don't think that it is something practically impossible and you might be in illusion, may be your degree of goodness was so high that you successfully made it to the soul. And from now on the walk in the process of life with the 'self' or the 'soul' will be so much better than before, filled with fairies and angels taking care of yours, enjoying to see you getting spoiled a bit by their overflowing love and nourishment.

Sometimes all we have to do is to surrender to the consciousness of the consciousness.

The SELF.

When we take some time to put ourselves into some kind of particular situations or when we face numerous varieties of situation- how we react? How we manage to handle them? What is our inbuilt tendency of working?

The exact manner in which we react to different things – our degree of happiness, irritation, excitement, numbness, dedication, fickleness, rigidity, flexibility, smartness and everything that comes into account of human nature; and also, those features uniquely present within us can be used to define our 'self' up to a certain proportion.

Then coming to the energies that we keep on attracting and repealing on the earth's surface. Those energies vary with the upgradation of 'me' on earth. Those are unseen forces that act on us because they have some purpose to fulfil as instructed by the divine or spirit guides based on our motto of life. They act, we react. But they are not so monopolistic on us. We might be feeling that they are such monopolistic but there is always some space for our free will which is the will of the 'self'.

To find the 'self' and get some relaxation on the working out of life in some negative or undesirable ways we have to find out and dig a research on the ingredients that constitute to give sense on our particular 'self'. We have to remove each covering on them with patience and love.

Usually with the fast flow of life we just flow with those driving forces. We hardly get some time form an analysis on how and why things are turning like this or like that.

Attempting to find the 'self' is necessary so that even if we are not able to manage those driving forces acting on us at least we can set a summary of-this is how this will turn into, this is how I can handle myself, these are the things related to it that I should stop thinking or expecting from , and what are those specific things that are going to work in favour of me. We can gradually get the exact idea of what are the favourable grounds for us in different aspects of life and also about those unfavourable one's. By performing such analysis, we can keep our 'self' away from being hopeless and ruining our own life by being the magnet of all negative forces around us. Let's turn our 'self' into the centre of all positive energies and let's be the example for people to believe again on the positive powers associated with them. Let's redefine the state of being hopeful on the grounds of relating or connecting with the 'self'. As being hopeful through this connection will turn out to be an everlasting one.

The 'self' is like a magical gift box there is so much of unlimited ideas associated with it. It is magical because it varies from person to person having unlimited theories of aligned energies and yet similar to the entire mankind. And it is a magical gift box because we have so much more to discover and it has so much to provide us every time, we unbox it.

Have faith on the 'self' more than anything else, as it has the capability to empower you like none other. It is your that loyal dog that will try to protect you even when you don't want to get protected. Discover the 'self' to achieve the heights that you have never dreamt of. Put your entire focus on words like delving deep into the self; connecting with the 'self'; exploring the 'self'; wandering within the 'self'. As though them you will make your way to your originality or authenticity. There you will be giving your expression like- "I am so talented! Wow!".

We can do wonders if we actually manage to reach out to the 'self'. Human mind has the ability to discover untold facts when it is brought into complete focus on one particular thing, let that thing be your 'self'. Make a perfect sketch of the 'self' in our mind so that we can appreciate its beauty at a regular interval, so that we can match our footsteps with it to perform a slow dance with elegance and ornament of divine rays present in us.

The 'self' is like a home given to us by the divine. We just have to add that secure and trustworthy feeling into it. We have to look at it with eyes filled with love and hope. Adore the way you set foots on ground of with different kinds of soil, adore the way you balance yourself before falling while walking or running, admire the way your body moves while dancing or even in general. Beautify the beauty within you.

No matter how much we try to be with the self after finding it out in our respective ways there will always be some phases of life where we will be set apart from it, and those are mostly the time of happiness. It is ok , but after you return don't leave out the essence of home associated with it. It will always be present on its respective place to provide that comfy shelter to you.

As like we are fond of decorating our house with so many mini and huge stuffs do that same with your 'self'. Those decorative stuffs here are like maintain-a good surrounding for you with energies those are much favourable on you, a good mental health equipped with better psychic abilities, a good physical health by having proper nutritious food not that boring type but you own type that suits your taste buds like heaven.

Find the beauty in the energies that your 'self' attracts, as it wishes to attract what we need, even if it is unpleasant, it is still working out for something good that you can have in some time.

Here I would like to put focus on the word 'thoughts'. Major part of the self is made up of thoughts. Thoughts that come to us from the beginning of the day to the end describes our 'self' in many obvious ways. Those are the clear reflections of the image of the 'self'. Keep a close eye on those thoughts to slowly find out the image of your 'self'. After relating or involving more with them work on that image to find out its perfect outline and figure.

It is so because as some specific kinds of thoughts keep on engaging our mind, they put their impact on our speech and instant formation of words at times. While they act on, our words, we exhibit certain rays through them, no doubt we always share our rays though our actions and reactions, but this exhibition of us inner thoughts through words allows us to see the 2d picture of our 'self'.

I want to add one more trusted way to find your true 'self', that way is self-dependency. It will work out to make us actually take the feel in 3d of how capable and trustworthy our 'self' is? Self-dependency can be used as a parameter to test our abilities and when we will do it for our own sake of self-improvement then it will be of great significance. Try depending on it happily and it won't disappoint you till the end of your journey.

Start taking steps closer to your 'self' after making a map of your own route to it. And slowly you will discover how eager your 'self' was to shower its love and affection on you. Feel the presence of it through each word that you mind has to say to you, through actions that you do subconsciously and consciously also but in the same way every time, through the new abilities that you discover as you put a test on its capability, through everything else that poses your uniqueness and even the common features. Admire the way your eyes look at your image in the mirror and admire how it admires your 'self'. Be that worm of self-admiration as we hardly get some time to admire our 'self' in the fast and furious race of survival among other humans.

Take some time out of your busy schedule or that social media stuffs to live for it, to feel that magical essence filled in the air in each moment that we got to spend on earth. Sometimes flow with the force and sometimes be with the 'self' either way, you are living it! Do it with happiness and live to the extreme, find joy in everything, make it euphoric, make it magical. Just don't pretend! Just don't act! Live it true! Be honestly happy with the 'self'.

Let's break the word myself into 'my' 'self' and let them protect each other.

Epilogue

Epilogue

This book wishes to lift up the mind of the reader and help them set free from negative energies or surroundings. It does not mean to create any offence to anyone or any particular community or individual. It makes the reader feel motivated and turn towards happiness through the means of realising the gifts of god. I am sorry if anyone have felt something bad while going through it, my only intention here is to spread the radiance of the divine on earth, to encourage people to keep up the good work and have faith in the grace. I wanted to make readers aware that they are precious as they are but changing for good is nothing to feel offended about. Rather changing for good, leads us towards the divine. It makes the divine feel proud as we are his children and a parent always feels proud by looking the way the child is trying to grow into a better human.

Let's accept positivity and spread positivity more in society. Let's learn to help and love others and ourselves with purity and good intentions. Let's spread humanity more by taking on and making ourselves feel the responsibility of things that we used to avoid earlier. Let's turn into responsible and good humans. Let's protect the left-over goodness and humanity on this planet with an intention to make it grow in future. The work of goodness that we will do on ourselves will instantly create its better impact on the society. Let's do it as a group and make the society a look alike place of that of heaven. Only we humans have the capability to change the entire look of earth, starting from the 'self' we will gradually turn the outlook of the planet. Yes, we hold that power and we are aware of it. And that's the reason why we are taking everything so lightly may it be about environmental issues or communal issues or anything else that is a matter of concern.

I have shared my ideas many of you might relate with it and some might not. We all have different ways of seeing and expressing things, I did what came to my mind during the course of writing. I respect everybody's ways of living life and I am not intending to interfere into the life of any individual. I would like it if my ideas get the normal respect of having a different perspective and not as provoking. As a common Indian girl, I have only used my freedom to express and write as per my will. If anywhere it seems as I am provoking then let me make it clear it is just in the form of direct address to the reader nothing more than that. I beg pardon and your understanding for the direct address is just a modern way of addressing the audience directly to make them feel more involved and letting them feel as if they are the one, which is absolutely not the case, it is just the way of creating pseudo feeling of connection. I wish you to read it for just the sake of fun and finding reason to be more happier than before.

I hope I was able to impart what I intended to. If even a single reader feels uplifted after being through the text, then, I will consider this attempt as a success. I hope I was able to make your days a bit more fun. I hope my book was able to add some joyous feelings in your everyday life, please do continue to be happy as it will make me happy.

We all know what tough phase we are going through now due to the covid situation; this is a writing to create some happiness in such hard times. We have to boots our mental health by being happy, we need to keep proceeding ahead with light heart and positivity within to avoid stress, unhappy feelings, depression and so many other negative vibrations within us or our surrounding. Let's be responsible citizens and follow the rules strictly and promise the divine to not to cause any severe harm to the environment or any individual in future that will annoy him or cause him pain in any way. As the divine loves us unlimitedly so it should be our first concern not to do any such thing that will make him upset.

Let's take care of the inner child more, let's look at ourselves more, let's protect the innocence of that child within us, let's be there to be with us. Whoever you are whatever you are doing if anything is tough for you don't think of losing hope the divine is making its way to help you, till then keep protecting yourself, keep loving yourself. Look at the unique ways through which the greater power loves us daily. Make it a daily habit of looking towards positivity, sometimes it might be really tough to do that due to some circumstance but that is the actual time when we need to take help from positive rays of divine. Let's turn into good or better than present, human beings and maintain that goodness until the end. Take the initiative to light up your life in your unique and good ways. Protect your originality with love and gentility. Let our hearts be safe in our own periphery of softly hard, rigidly flexible and gently tough features.

A ray of hope, a ray of sunlight, a ray of moonlight, a ray of starlight, whatever you want to name this, name it in your way and make this a happy place for you.

A shelter for a nomad, a hope for the hopeless, a form of root for the rootless, an address for the lost, a home for the homeless, a wand for your magic, a sense of relief for your tensed mind, a touch of petal on your cheek, a fragrance of divinity on earth, a rose from me to you with a loving smile.

Let that light, guide you right.

9 798889 753476

Printed by Libri Plureos GmbH in Hamburg,
Germany